ZONDERVAN

Everyday Holy

Copyright © 2018 by Melanie Shankle

This title is also available as a Zondervan ebook.

This title is also available as a Zondervan audio book.

Requests for information should be addressed to:

Zondervan, *3900 Sparks Dr. SE, Grand Rapids, Michigan 49546*

Library of Congress Cataloging-in-Publication Data
ISBN 978-0-310346685

The author is represented by Alive Literary Agency, 7680 Goddard Street, Suite 200, Colorado Springs, Colorado 80920, www.aliveliterary.com.

Art direction: Adam Hill

Interior design: Lori Lynch

Printed in China

18 19 20 21 22 DSC 10 9 8 7 6 5 4 3 2 1

EVERYDAY

HOLY

FINDING A BIG GOD
IN THE LITTLE MOMENTS

100 DEVOTIONS

Melanie Shankle

ZONDERVAN
.com

INTRODUCTION

If someone had told me that one day I'd write a devotional, I would have taken to my bed and told them they had clearly mistaken me for someone much more spiritually and scripturally astute. Devotions are supposed to be written by people like Oswald Chambers and use words like *thou* and *beseech*. If I use any of those words in this book, it will only be thanks to the fact that I am currently addicted to *The Crown* on Netflix.

But as I thought and prayed over the idea of this devotional project, I realized that God speaks to us all in different ways, using little pieces of our lives to show us His love, mercy, provision, and grace. And that is what you'll find in these pages—little pieces that point us to a big God. I beseech you to make it part of your daily routine as thou strivest to know Him more.

Day 1

GOD IS NOT OLD

....

He has made everything beautiful in its time. He has
also set eternity in the human heart; yet no one can
fathom what God has done from beginning to end.

ECCLESIASTES 3:11

Over the last month, I've felt fear and worry well up in me time and time again. And I don't really talk about it because it's not fun to talk about. I'd rather think about cute shoes, my hair, and that everything is 40 percent off at Gap right now.

The important things.

I think I'm beginning to realize that we never really arrive at some incredible destination of perfect peace and tranquillity. It's a daily dependence on God, trusting and knowing that He can meet all my needs and has a great plan for my life. I know it, yet I'm quick to fall into my old patterns and forget.

I've thought so much about Paul's words in Philippians: "Not that I have already obtained all this, or have already arrived at my goal, but I press on to take hold of that for which Christ Jesus took hold of me" (3:12).

I'm quick to get bogged down in the what-ifs, to worry and fret over things that are ultimately out of my control anyway, to try to come up with my own solutions and totally discount His sovereignty in all situations.

I worry that I'll regret not having another baby. I wonder if Caroline will grow up to be happy and normal without a sibling. Who will she roll her eyes when I say embarrassing things? Which is inevitable, by the way.

I worry about our finances and if we're going to owe money to the IRS this year. I worry that we're not saving enough for the future. I worry that our property taxes are going to go through the roof now that our neighbors have built the Taj Mahal next door.

I worry about Perry and me flying somewhere together because what if something happens? I worry about Caroline and if I'm raising her to the best of my ability. I have days when my patience reaches its limit. And then I feel guilty.

And then I worry about feeling guilty.

I worry because I'm speaking to a group of women in a few weeks and I don't know if I'll have anything to say beyond, "Hey, y'all. What's up?" What if I fail? What if I screw it all up? What if I've heard God wrong?

So *basically*, on some days I'm the definition of a mess.

I've just given you a lot of information right there. I feel a little like that episode of *Seinfeld* where George bares his soul to Jerry and then says, "That is who I am and everything I am capable of."

My point is that I don't have it all together, and I have days that just really stink. But I try not to focus on those things because, most of the time, I try to refrain from hosting my own party full of woe and pity.

A few weeks ago, I sat across the room from our former housekeeper, Cata. She is sixty-seven years old and has cleaned houses for most of her life. A month earlier, she and her husband lost their home and much of what they owned in a house fire. They have no insurance. Yet I sat there and listened to Cata tell me in broken English how blessed she felt and how God has been faithful to provide help throughout her entire ordeal. She looked at me with joy in her eyes and said, "Melanie, God is not old. He is still working."

How much do I love that she said, "God is not old"? It totally makes me think of when God asks Moses, "Is the Lord's arm too short?" (Numbers 11:23).

God is not too old, and His arm is not too short.

I've been in a season of life where I often feel easily overwhelmed. After my conversation with Cata, I got on my knees and prayed about all my fears, doubts, and worries. *Why don't I trust You the way I should? Why do I go back to that place of relying on my own power? Why do I let fear overtake me? When will I be the person I wish I could be?*

I didn't get an answer.

But a few days later, I was walking my dogs down to an empty field by our house to let them run. I stood there watching them and noticed one lone bluebonnet sprouting up in the middle of the field. I know from past years that in another week, the entire field will be covered in bluebonnets. But for now, there is just that one.

I felt God say to me in the still, small place in my heart, "My girl, that's how it is sometimes. After a long winter, spring doesn't happen all at once. It happens one flower at a time. I make all things beautiful, one flower at a time." And that was the reminder I needed that God is not old. He is always at work, even when it may not seem obvious at first.

Day 2

YOU AREN'T THE
MOST RIGHT

....

If I speak in the tongues of men or of angels, but do not have
love, I am only a resounding gong or a clanging cymbal.

1 CORINTHIANS 13:1

You know what I'm tired of right now? Watching Christians eat their own. I'm talking about all the attacking and backbiting and endless arguments over what Jesus said and how He said it and who is right and who is wrong. I will never claim to be a great theologian, largely because I am not a great theologian, but I believe in a God who loves mercy and grace. I believe in a God who tells us that without love we are just clanging cymbals.

I believe when we dissect the Word of God for the purpose of arguing with others over who is the most right, it makes God sad. I think He shakes His holy head and wonders how we are missing the entire point of Christianity while eating lunch and going to work and grocery shopping with people all around who don't know Him. Instead of showing them who He is and extending grace and understanding and mercy and love, we fight, argue, and judge each other.

Don't get me wrong. I believe we're called to examine God's Word and know it, to be able to give an answer for what we believe and why we believe it. But when we use that knowledge to belittle others or condemn them? NO, MA'AM.

> For this very reason, make every effort to add to your faith goodness; and to goodness, knowledge; and to knowledge, self-control; and to self-control, perseverance; and to perseverance, godliness; and to godliness, mutual affection; and to mutual affection, love. For if you possess these qualities in increasing measure, they will keep you from being ineffective and unproductive in your knowledge of our Lord Jesus Christ. (2 Peter 1:5–8)

I think Satan (oh yes, I just dropped in a *Satan* like I'm the church lady) loves when we get so distracted by these small debates, so inwardly focused, that we forget about the world around us—hurting, hopeless, and lost. A world that is desperate for something that looks different, something that offers a hope and a future that's different from the wreckage of the past and present.

I have lived a large chunk of my forty-something years in rebellion against God. I've ignored His Word, run from His love, and tried my best to screw up my life with a lot of wrong decisions. I've also spent many years devoted to Him to the point of becoming legalistic and judgmental and losing the joy of my salvation. I've looked at a lot of specks in other people's eyes while ignoring the big ol' plank in my own.

But somewhere over the last several years, I've begun to realize that my small mind can't comprehend the love and mercy of God. He is not a one-size-fits-all Creator. He is the God of the Universe, and He has made us all uniquely different and equipped each of us with gifts and abilities to fulfill the plans He has for us. Why would we assume that our walks with Him or even our understanding of Him would look the same? As Isaiah 40:13 says, "Who can fathom the Spirit of the LORD, or instruct the LORD his counselor?"

My walk with Christ is as uniquely mine as my personality. I've spent a lot of time believing I should be more like this Bible teacher or more emotional like that person or hear from God in a certain way or adopt a child from Africa or sell all my earthly possessions—but God has made me to be me. And He's made you to be you. If God were after only one type of relationship with one type of person, it would've been a whole lot easier for Him to create just one person and be done with it.

I speak from experience. I only have one child, and it's easy to know her because she's the only one I have.

But I know from watching my friends with multiple children that they have unique relationships with each of their kids based on their personalities and gifts. They talk to each of their kids differently and show them love in ways that speak to that child.

I believe God is the same way.

And I believe it's ignorant to think that our understanding of Him is the only way and there's no room for growth. I don't think any of us will get to heaven and receive a trophy or a plaque with "YOU WERE THE MOST RIGHT" engraved on it. Throughout my life, God has been my Redeemer, Protector, Provision, Salvation, Lover, and Friend. He has caused conviction when I am in the wrong, and He has loved me lavishly and extravagantly when I am simply His child in need of grace and mercy.

I am not a Bible scholar. I can't tell you the Greek and Hebrew translations for specific words. In fact, I just bought a fancy Bible a few weeks ago with the Greek and Hebrew translations, and I'm sure it will be great as soon as I learn how to use it. I'll keep you posted.

Here's what I do know: I do not want to serve a God who fits into my limited understanding. I don't want to serve a God who can be completely explained in the human realm. I want a God who is so much bigger than me that I'll spend the rest of my life trying to know Him more, love Him more, and serve Him better.

I believe in a God who removes my sins as far as the east is from the west—because that's a distance my mind can't comprehend. To me, that's a God who is worth my devotion. That's a God I want to share with a lost world instead of reducing Him to what my limited human perspective can understand.

It makes me think of a scene in *Prince Caspian* by C. S. Lewis. Lucy sees Aslan after a long time apart and exclaims, "Aslan! You're bigger."

> "That is because you are older, little one," answered he.
> "Not because you are?"
>   "I am not. But every year you grow you will find me bigger."

I pray that every year we grow we will find Him bigger.

VEGGIES MADE ME CRY

For we are God's handiwork, created in Christ Jesus to do
good works, which God prepared in advance for us to do.

EPHESIANS 2:10

A Snoodle's Tale" is an episode of *Veggie Tales*. I'm not necessarily a *Veggie Tales* fan. I have issues with their lack of hands and feet . . . yet their incredible ability to wield a sword and, well, *walk*. But many years ago, Caroline was watching *Veggie Tales,* an episode about a creature called the Snoodle Doo. It spoke to me so deeply that I started to cry.

The veggies made me cry.

Yes, the tears may have been partially due to my ongoing hormonal imbalance, but it went deeper than that.

The story of the Snoodle Doo is about finding out who you are and who God created you to be. It's about letting go of all the false, hurtful things people have said to you and about you. It's about seeing yourself through God's eyes.

In the video, the Snoodle Doo gets so weighed down by everyone's perception of him, but then he finds his Creator, who draws a picture of who the Snoodle Doo really is, who he was created to be. The Snoodle Doo asks, "Is that me? I want to believe it, but I'm afraid to."

The Creator replies, "I know who you are. I made you. I've seen you fall down in the mud and the goo. I've seen all you have done and all you will do. I gave you your pack, your paints, and your wings. I chose them for you; they're your special things."

And it was at that point that I got a little teary.

I'd spent so many years letting my past dictate who I thought I was. Every mistake and bad decision I'd made defined me. I didn't feel like I deserved anything good. I felt like He had saved me and that was enough.

I was afraid to tell anyone my hopes and dreams because I thought they were out of reach. I didn't think I had any real talents or abilities, and even if I did, I didn't know what they were or how they could be used.

I was going to spend my life being a less than mediocre pharmaceutical drug rep and hopefully an at least average wife and mother.

But He had and has so much more in store. For me and for you.

Psalm 139 says that we are wonderfully and fearfully made. Psalm 17:8 says we are the apple of His eye. Psalm 18:19 says He rescued me because He delights in me. Isaiah 49:16 says He has engraved me on the palms of His hands. Zephaniah 3:17 says He takes great delight in me. He will quiet me with His love and rejoice over me with singing.

That is some serious love. That is a God who wants to give us hope and a future. That is a God who sees us as His masterpiece.

He made each of us with specific plans and purposes in mind. He gave us talents, gifts, and abilities that are unique to us. It's our job to find and use them.

When we keep our eyes on Him and His vision for us, we will know what it is to soar.

And soaring is never boring. (I'm sorry for rhyming. [No, I'm not.] I blame the residual effect of the Bob the Tomato.)

Day 4

FOR THIS DAY

....

"I will lead the blind by ways they have not known, along
unfamiliar paths I will guide them; I will turn the darkness
into light before them and make the rough places smooth."

ISAIAH 42:16

I believe it was New Year's Eve 1995, when Perry and I were dating and broke up because he wouldn't come home from the ranch to celebrate a "fake holiday." My best friend, Gulley, and I ended up spending it together. We ate way too much Italian food and stayed up way too late, which is my only excuse for how many times I belted out Faith Hill's "It Matters to Me." I felt like it best summed up my feelings about Perry's New Year's Eve apathy. It wasn't my favorite New Year's Eve celebration. I bet Gulley doesn't remember that year as her favorite New Year's celebration either.

To make it worse, Perry shot a nice ten-point buck on New Year's Day, which only served to confirm in his mind that he made the right choice. And these days I tend to agree with him that big New Year's celebrations are overrated. In fact, this past year we received an invitation to an unbelievably fancy New Year's Eve party. The invitation was hand-delivered. In a box. With a beaded chandelier inside the box. The attire was couture/black tie, and we turned it down. Because these days we prefer non-couture flannel. And watching bowl games. And getting to bed by 10:30 P.M.

But I vividly remember celebrating New Year's Eve of 2007, mainly because I'd never been so glad to see a year come to an end. For me, 2007 was a year of incredible transition. If someone had sat me down in January of 2007 and told me all the things that year would bring, I think I may have curled up in the fetal position and stayed there for the next twelve months. It was a year that refined my faith in ways I didn't even know it needed to be refined. It was essentially a twelve-month process of God stripping away everything in which I'd tried to find security. In January, I was faced with false allegations that made me fear I'd lose my job, and just the thought of that possibility sent me into near hysteria (or if I'm being completely honest, full-blown hysteria). The allegations were proven false, but then some other things happened along the way that led Perry and me to make the decision that I would resign in April.

The pharmaceutical job I'd held for ten years was gone. The income, the company car, the benefits were gone. I consoled myself with how well Perry's business was doing and how much money we had in various accounts. We were totally fine. And then Perry's best employee ended up going to jail (it's a long story), which slowed down the progress they were able to make on various jobs. Shortly thereafter, Perry's back went out again and we knew he was going to need surgery.

Our new insurance didn't want to pay on some of the claims, which left us with medical bills higher than we'd expected; the brakes went out on Perry's truck; we had to get some major dental work done; and finally, someone broke out my car window right before Christmas. We began to joke that we might as well just start flushing hundred-dollar bills down the toilet because it was a more efficient way to drain our bank account.

The Bible study I'd done that fall was *A Woman's Heart* by Beth Moore. Week 2 of the study was about taking risks and inviting God to do His will to grow us. I knew immediately that God was calling me to take that risk. And I didn't want to because I was scared.

But I did it. And you need to know that I did it with much fear and trembling.

I had no idea what was going to happen, but I knew that I had lost some of my passion for Him, and I wanted it back. Ultimately, my need was stronger than my fear. Which means I had A LOT of need, because my fear usually outweighs most everything.

And that's when the bottom fell out. Honestly, it was almost comically apparent what God was trying to show me about myself. I have often been so guilty of finding security in the things this world offers. It's not even that I love money so much or have to have it; I just like the security it offers. I felt like as long as our bank account had a certain balance, then everything would be okay.

The irony is that *A Woman's Heart* follows the Israelites as Moses leads them out of Egypt and to the Promised Land. I spent a lot of time being like the Israelites, grumbling to myself, "I don't know why God led me away from my job and all that security if He's just going to hang us out to dry like this." But then God reminded me how He provided manna for the children of Israel every morning. He gave them what they needed for that day. Their security had to be in Him and in His provision. FOR THAT DAY. And that's what He's promised us: He will give us what we need for this day.

His provision doesn't hinge on what the bank says or what the stock market does or who the president may be. He is over all those things, and He is faithful and just to provide. I spent 2007 being refined like never before, but I can also say I drew closer to Him than ever. When all the fears and worries began to rise up, I learned to run to Him instead of adding up bills in my head and trying to come up with my own solution.

In 2007, God led me into a new land. It was a year of me questioning what I believe and how much I believe it. Of learning that it's okay to ask Him to help me overcome my unbelief. Of literally putting my money where my mouth is or, more accurately, where my heart is. Of learning to trust in Him in ways that I have never trusted before. It was one of the hardest, most challenging times of my life, and I still wrestle with some of these same things, but I know that He that began a good work in me and will carry it on to completion.

And as I completed my Bible study of Moses and the tabernacle that fall, I learned something that I had never realized before still resonates with me. From the time Moses led the Israelites out of Egypt, through all the grumbling in the desert, through all the hardships, to the completion of the tabernacle, one year had passed.

ONE YEAR.

How is it even possible that all of that happened in one year? As Beth wrote, "It had been the worst year of his life and the best year of his life."

I feel you, Moses. I think that's how I'll always remember 2007. The best and the worst. But I know that, like Moses, I wouldn't trade it for anything.

HELLO, GOD. IT'S ME, MELANIE

Give thanks to the Lord for his unfailing
love and his wonderful deeds.

PSALM 107:8

Several years ago, I was watching a Barbara Walters special. (I *know*. But Barbara Walters is my kryptonite. I cannot resist the way she never fails to make a celebrity cry.) She was interviewing Ellen DeGeneres. I've always liked Ellen. I remember first seeing her on Comedy Central and thinking she was hysterical. I love her dry humor, her warmth, and her style. And don't even get me started on how much I love her as the voice of Dory in *Finding Nemo*. If you haven't occasionally reminded yourself to "just keep swimming" then I'm not sure we can be friends.

Anyway, Ellen was talking about the ups and downs of her career and her life. She has had some huge successes, but some really painful things have also happened along the way. At one point, they showed a clip of her first appearance on *The Tonight Show* with Johnny Carson, where she did a great bit about calling God on the phone.

At the end of the interview, Barbara Walters asked Ellen what she would say to God if she really could call Him on the phone, and Ellen got teary-eyed (this is what I'm saying—it never fails) and replied with such sincerity, "I'd say thank You. I've got nothing but gratitude. My whole life, I'm so blessed. I'm so lucky and I feel it every day." Her words convicted me so much that I turned off the TV, and that is serious.

I don't know Ellen's religious beliefs. That's not the point. The point is her overwhelming gratitude. She recognizes her blessings. It made me ask myself if I'm as quick to recognize my blessings or if I get consumed with what I don't have?

When I pray, which is really the same as a phone call to God, how much time do I spend thanking Him for all He has already done in my life? Do I tell Him that I realize He's blessed me more than I deserve and that if He never did one thing for me other than sending His son two thousand years ago to die on a cross, that's more than I could ever repay?

I would never call my friends every day and say, "Let me tell you what you can do for me today." I'm betting if I did, it wouldn't be long before they started screening my calls. When someone does something nice for me, I am quick to tell them thank you. That's just good manners. I'd never say, "Well, that's n-i-i-ice, but if you really want to help . . ."

As a mom, I have always spent lots of time reminding Caroline to say thank you. I tell her that's what nice people do. We say thank you when people do something for us so they know they're appreciated. It's common courtesy.

Why am I so quick to thank the cashier at the grocery store for finding a coupon but so slow to thank God for giving me the air I breathe, the family I love, and the life that is so much more than I deserve?

I never thought I'd say that watching a Barbara Walters special caused me to have a spiritual revelation, but it did. Ellen's words caused me to stop and remember that sometimes nothing makes you more aware of what you've been given than taking the time to say thank you.

Day 6

BUILDING WITH WEEK THINGS

....

The LORD had said to Abram, "Go from your country, your
people and your father's household to the land I will show
you. I will make you into a great nation, and I will bless you;
I will make your name great, and you will be a blessing."

GENESIS 12:1–2

Sometimes when circumstances get too big or seem to be different from what I want, doubts start creeping in. *What if this isn't the right thing? What if I heard God wrong? What if I've made a huge mistake? What if I'm totally screwing up my child and she ends up living in a van down by the river?*

I get scared. I realize this doesn't make me different from anyone else. We all like to feel in control of every aspect of our lives, and it's hard to surrender that control. It's hard to say, "I trust You"—no matter what.

One of the few constants in life is that things will always change. And I, like many others, hate change. It leaves me feeling unsettled, unsure, and insecure as I try to find new footing in different circumstances. But the thing about moving forward is that it requires venturing into new, uncharted territory.

Often, I feel a little like God is holding a big megaphone and saying, "Hey, you! YES, YOU OF LITTLE FAITH. *I have a plan.*"

Abram had no idea what God had in store for him. His mind couldn't imagine what God was going to do. Yet he packed up his camels, his turbans, and what-have-you, loaded up the family, and headed toward a strange land. He was the original *Grapes of Wrath* story. What made him do it? His faith. His faith that God wasn't going to do him wrong. His faith that God wasn't going to lead him to a place with no provision for him and his family. His faith in God's promises.

What if Abram had stayed? What if he had decided that the whole venture was just a little too risky? What if he chose to stick with what was familiar? I don't know the answer to all of that, other than knowing that God wouldn't have been able to use him the way He did. Sure, God has a destiny for all of us, a plan that He has known since before we took a breath, but He never forces us to do anything. We take our own steps, whether they are toward His will or away from it.

The thing that's scary is that the steps toward His will are the hardest of all because they require us to leave the familiar. Wasn't it Loretta Lynn who said something like, "Better the devil you know than the devil you don't"? And yes, I just quoted Loretta Lynn. Bear with me because this isn't the first time and certainly won't be the last.

It's all about faith. "By faith Abraham, when called to go to a place he would later receive as his inheritance, obeyed and went, even though he did not know where he was going" (Hebrews 11:8). Hebrews 11 even goes on to say how God used Abraham even though "he was as good as dead" (v. 12). I'm not great, but I'm certainly better than practically dead.

Anyway, that's how I feel. I'm not sure where life is headed, but I know God has a plan. The voice of destiny is ultimately the voice of God. Do we believe that? Do we believe that He cares about our seemingly insignificant lives that much? Do we believe that God sees the value in us?

The Sunday school answer is yes, but the reality is deeper than that. Sometimes as we watch God put pieces of our life together like a puzzle, the question that gnaws away at us is "Who am *I* to deserve any of this?" I'm so flawed and so weak. Some days my faith wouldn't even rate as average. I relate all too well to the man who asked Jesus to heal his son in Mark 9:23–24. Jesus told him every-thing is possible for him who believes, and the father exclaimed, "I do believe; help me overcome my unbelief!"

It makes me laugh because of how much I relate. How many times have I done the same thing—professed how much I believe and then prayed to overcome all my doubts in the same breath? Too many to count. Seriously. I am a weak vessel.

But so was Abraham. And Moses. And King David. They all had moments of doubt, moments when they took matters into their own hands and tried their best to screw everything up. Yet God had amazing plans for them. He used them despite their human limitations. Only God can do that. Only He can take the weak things of this world and use them for His plans and purposes.

He is the architect and the builder. Our job is to take the step of faith, away from what we know and away from the false security we cling to, toward what He is building with our lives. He never promised it would be easy, and He certainly never promised it would be on our timetable; He just promised that with Him all things are possible and He'll be with us always.

Day 7

I BELIEVE

....

For to us a child is born, to us a son is given, and
the government will be on his shoulders. And
he will be called Wonderful Counselor, Mighty
God, Everlasting Father, Prince of Peace.

ISAIAH 9:6

About two days after Christmas last year, my daughter, Caroline, told me she had something serious she needed to discuss. If you're a mom, you know that nothing truly strikes terror in your heart more than your child needing to have a "serious discussion." As it turned out, she confessed that she no longer believed in Santa Claus, and truth be told, she'd known even before she caught me moving that stupid Elf on a Shelf a few weeks earlier. (The Elf on a Shelf has to be one of the dumbest marketing ploys Americans have ever bought into. How can we make Christmas more stressful? Oh, *I know!* Let's get a fake elf that is supposed to do whimsical things every night like take a bath in a tub of marshmallows or zip line with the Barbie dolls!)

But Caroline had held on because she wasn't quite ready to let go of that part of childhood. I totally get it. Something in us longs to believe in something bigger than what our eyes can see. A few weeks earlier, our little family of three had spent the afternoon watching *The Polar Express* while a fire roared in the fireplace and the lights twinkled on the Christmas tree. It was one of those sweet, unplanned moments that takes you by surprise yet is now etched in my mind as one of my favorite memories.

I kind of dozed off as we watched the movie because I've seen it a million times. Plus I was a little tired from all the late nights moving the Elf on a Shelf. But when the part came on where the kids arrive at the North Pole, I made myself stay awake because it's one of my favorite scenes. In my imagination, if a North Pole full of elves and Santa were to exist, it would look exactly like it does in *The Polar Express*.

At one point, the little boy is standing in the midst of all the elves who are overcome with excitement at the prospect of Santa Claus's appearance. Everyone is cheering, the reindeer are jumping up and down, and the elves come out with these huge reins of solid jingle bells. The little boy begins to look puzzled. He can tell he's missing something that the rest of the crowd is hearing and experiencing. About that time, the little girl next to him whispers, "Aren't those bells the most beautiful sound?" It confirms what he already knows: something is lacking.

When I watched that scene, it made me wonder how many people out there know something is missing. They have the beautifully decorated tree. They have the wrapped packages tied up with pretty bows. They have a turkey thawing in the refrigerator and family that will gather around a table.

They may even go to church on Christmas Eve and listen as the people around them sing and celebrate the birth of a baby born over two thousand years ago. And they'll sit there and wonder what's missing.

I know how that feels because I spent a lot of years feeling that same way. I grew up in church. I was there every time the doors were open, but something was missing. I'd hear people talk about what God had done for them and the difference He'd made in their life, and I just didn't feel it. And it wasn't because of lack of desire. I wanted to know Him, but I didn't know how.

Years of listening to sermons and going to church camp had given me glimpses, but I wanted more. As the little boy watches the bells he can't hear, he hears the crowd roar as Santa appears, and he stands there and says, "I can't see him! I can't see him!" That's how I felt for so long. I couldn't see Him.

Finally, in desperation, the little boy closes his eyes, grabs the jingle bell that has fallen to the ground at his feet, and says, "I believe. I believe. I believe." And at that moment, he hears the bell ring and Santa appears right behind him.

Sometimes it takes a leap of faith.

Because no matter how much everyone around that little boy believed in Santa and saw him clearly, he had to see him for himself. He had to believe even when part of him wanted to hold on to logic and reason. Logic and reason don't require much faith. They may keep you from looking foolish, but they can also keep you from going on the greatest adventure of your life.

Fifteen years ago, I reached a point of desperation. After all those years in church, I had to see Him for myself. It didn't matter what my preacher said or what my friends experienced. I needed to take a leap and let Him pour out His grace and mercy on my life. Then one night, in the middle of a Bible study surrounded by people who were experiencing something I wanted, I closed my eyes as tears fell down my cheeks and whispered, "I believe. I believe. I believe."

And life has never been the same.

A virgin birth. Angels appearing to a field full of shepherds. Wise men following a star from the east. The Son of God sent to save us from our sins.

It doesn't make sense until you see Him for yourself and He is there. Waiting for those who will take the leap and believe.

Day 8

CHARIOTS, HORSES, AND OTHER THINGS THAT DON'T MATTER

Some trust in chariots and some in horses, but
we trust in the name of the LORD our God.

PSALM 20:7

Sometimes I have this realization that I am putting a huge amount of trust in myself. I am counting on my abilities, my charm, my intellect, and my resources to help me get through certain situations instead of trusting God. (I'm not saying I have an overabundance of any of these things, which makes it that much sadder that they're what I'm relying on.) I spend a lot of time worrying and trying to figure out how to handle certain circumstances and totally discount what God may have to say about the matter.

I mean, really. He's only the Creator of the universe and knows minor details like the number of hairs on my head and stars in the sky. How could He *possibly* know about my huge problems here on earth? What does He know about navigating a daughter through her teens? That kind of mentality should make you feel a bit sorry for me, considering I've been counting on my own intellect (and if *that* train of thought doesn't show how limited my intellect is, I don't know what does).

But then I remember something I heard one time: "Don't judge circumstances by what we see but by what He says." I've held on to it ever since. What are any of our earthly problems compared to the unsurpassed sovereignty of what He says?

Another way I've heard this thought expressed is that trusting in God is believing in His heart when you can't see His hand. It's easy to believe in His goodness when all is right with our world, but what about when everything *isn't* all right? What then?

It helps me to stop and remember that the God who led Moses, the God who protected Daniel in the lions' den, and the God who kept Shadrach, Meshach, and Abednego from burning alive is fully capable of handling our problems right here in the twenty-first century. He has seen it all and He rules over all.

He's still mighty, He's still on the throne, and He's still leading His people where He wants them to go, even when the path looks scary and dark. He knows the way even when all we see is darkness and fear. And when we stop looking to ourselves and look to Him, He will show us the way.

The challenge is to quit looking at the strength we think the "chariots and horses" in our lives can give us—our own instincts, talents, and abilities—and to start trusting in Him, remembering that He holds the answers in the palm of His hand.

Day 9

SCARED MONKEYS

....

Have I not commanded you? Be strong and courageous.
Do not be afraid; do not be discouraged, for the
Lord your God will be with you wherever you go.

JOSHUA 1:9

I read a joke the other day that went something like this:

> God to the angels: "Look! I have created man!"
> Angels: "You messed up a perfectly good monkey is what you've done! Look how anxious and fearful that thing is."

It made me laugh because it's so true. We are fearful creatures. Even those of us who seem to be brave are usually just better at hiding how terrified we really are by certain situations or potential outcomes. But you know what I love? That God knows how scared we feel and uses us for His purposes anyway.

I once read that the phrase "Do not fear" or "Fear not" is used 365 times throughout the Bible. I have no idea if that's true or not because the premise is way too close to a mathematical word problem for my comfort. (Talk about fear! Let's discuss algebra.) But I do know that throughout the Word of God, His people are constantly being reassured that God is with them, that He goes before them and behind them, and that He holds them in His righteous right hand.

There will never be a time in our lives when there isn't some potential obstacle or situation to be afraid of. In *The Wizard of Oz*, the Cowardly Lion spends his entire journey searching for courage, and when he finally meets the Great Wizard of Oz, he is told, "There is no living thing that is not afraid when it faces danger. The true courage is in facing danger when you are afraid, and that kind of courage you have in plenty."

I have no doubt that Joshua was terrified as the time grew near for him to lead the people of Israel across the Jordan River and into the Promised Land. I'm sure he was filled with concerns about whether he'd heard God correctly and whether he was man enough to fill the enormous shoes Moses had left behind. (I so want to make a joke here about how Moses' shoes never wore out in the wilderness. Nerdy Bible humor for the win.)

But God assured Joshua: "No one will be able to stand up against you all the days of your life. As I was with Moses, so I will be with you; I will never leave you or forsake you" (Joshua 1:5). And God promises us the same. Fearful times will come, scary circumstances will arise, giants will stand in our way, but we have a God who is with us always, whispering that true courage is when we walk ahead in our fear, let go of the reins, take the leap of faith, always knowing that He promises to never leave us or forsake us.

Day 10

THE HIGHLIGHTS REEL

We will not compare ourselves with each other
as if one of us were better and another worse.
We have far more interesting things to do
with our lives. Each of us is an original.

GALATIANS 5: 26 THE MESSAGE

I love social media. I mean, *clearly*. I've had a blog since 2006, which was essentially the dawn of the internet and really forward-thinking for a person who as recently as 1998 declared that email would really never take off as a viable form of communication.

But I think an interesting phenomenon has happened as we've begun to document our lives on Facebook, Twitter, Instagram, Snapchat, and whatever has been invented while I typed this sentence: we've never had so many ways to compare our lives to other people. We know what our friends are eating for breakfast, if they're drinking a fruity drink on a beach in Mexico, when their kids make the honor roll, and—help me—we've seen photos of feet at more locations than anyone ever needs to see. All the feelings of inferiority we used to feel just when everyone's Christmas newsletter arrived are now available to us every day via our phones, tablets, and computers.

We can begin to feel guilty that some girl we went to high school with sets up a hot chocolate bar for her kids after school while we just yelled at ours and threatened to drop them off at the fire station if they complain about their algebra homework. Hypothetically speaking.

It can look like everyone's house is prettier, meals taste better, husbands are more romantic, and kids are smarter than ours. We can get caught in this never-ending loop of comparison, and nothing makes me feel more unsettled. There's a reason for the famous quote "Comparison is the thief of joy," because you can always come up short in your own mind when you lose sight of your blessings while counting what someone else has—or at least what they appear to have.

Because social media is just a snapshot of our life. A quick, beautiful, fleeting moment that is well filtered and often not very indicative of real life, which may involve a dog throwing up on the kitchen floor and dinner burning and the fact that your husband is on your actual last nerve.

We all have unique gifts, callings, joys, and sorrows. Life is too short for comparison, and it only hurts us to focus on what we don't have instead. We need to walk our road and not spend time looking left and right to see what everyone else is doing, especially because we never know the road someone else. Sometimes, when you look beneath the surface, things aren't always what they appear. People may be hurting even when it all looks shiny on the outside.

Let's encourage each other to be the best version of who God has called us to be and cheer each other on in our victories and successes and be honest with each other when we have failed and feel inadequate and are hurting. That's how you build real relationships. Plus, God has far more interesting things for us to do than to spend our time comparing our lives to someone else. Embrace the gifts you've been given, and walk your road with the security that can only come from God.

Day 11

MELANIE DOESN'T SHARE BED

....

As soon as he had finished speaking to Saul, the
soul of Jonathan was knit to the soul of David,
and Jonathan loved him as his own soul.

1 SAMUEL 18:1 ESV

My friend Jen grew up in the Dallas area, and when we were all in college, she invited us to stay at her dad's house for the weekend. We arrived at the house late Friday night, and it quickly became apparent that there weren't enough beds for everyone. This is the kind of attention to detail that college girls lack when playing hostess.

So without even thinking twice about it, a girl named Gulley and I declared that we were happy to share a twin bed for the weekend. And here's the thing: I meant it. And I don't think you can fully appreciate the momentous nature of this unless I make you aware of my myriad sleep issues. I need about six pillows at all times, the temperature has to be just right, and the sheets have to be pulled tight and preferably made out of a cotton that would make angel wings jealous. You know that episode of *Friends* when Joey Tribbiani declares, "Joey doesn't share food"? That's me. Except with a bed. I don't share bed. Even after almost twenty years of marriage, my husband and I sleep under different sets of covers, as far apart as possible.

It's very romantic.

But I was willing to share a twin bed with Gulley, who has now been my best friend for over twenty-five years. We climbed into that bed and spent the rest of the night not even pretending to sleep but instead laughing and whispering as we shared stories about our families, our ex-boyfriends, and the experiences that were shaping the women we were trying to become at nineteen years old. I look back on that weekend as the weekend when I knew I'd found a kindred spirit.

You hear so many people talk about finding their soul mates only in relation to who they marry, but I think that as women, our real soul mates are often found when we recognize some version of ourselves in another woman. Gulley and I were both children of divorce; we knew what it was like to be shuttled back and forth on weekends and all the emotional landmines that lie therein. We had been hurt by girlfriends we'd trusted. We found humor in the same quirky things and shared a love of novelty rap songs. Maybe it's where we were in life, with the wide-eyed innocence of girls on the brink of adulthood. Whatever the circumstances, we were vulnerable with each other in that way you are when you know you've found someone you can completely trust with your heart.

It was like each of us went into the friendship with an awareness of how the other had been hurt and disappointed in the past, and there was an unspoken vow that we would do our best to see that we never caused each other pain. We saw each other's fragility masked in a brave exterior and began to make each other stronger people than we'd been before.

I've loved the Bible story about the friendship between Jonathan and David ever since the days when I learned about it on the flannel board in Sunday school, but when I read it as an adult, I noticed that it talks about their souls being knit together. That's a powerful bond (and I don't really even understand how knitting works). It's clear that Jonathan didn't work to knit his soul to David's but that God absolutely showed up in that moment to forever weave their hearts and souls together. What God knew at that moment—which neither Jonathan nor David could have envisioned—was how much they would need each other in the years to come. God brought them together at a point when he knew they would both serve to make the other a stronger man than he would have been alone.

Here's a little-known fact about Gulley and me. We were delivered by the same doctor at the same hospital in Houston, Texas, almost exactly one year apart. For the next eighteen years, our lives took twists and turns and moved us in all kinds of directions, but I believe that God always knew He was going to bring us together at exactly the time we'd need each other the most, and it would be His gift to us for the rest of our lives.

Day 12

JUST ASK

....

"Ask, and it will be given to you; seek, and you will
find; knock, and it will be opened to you. For everyone
who asks receives, and the one who seeks finds,
and to the one who knocks it will be opened."

MATTHEW 7:7–8 ESV

Several years ago, I realized I had, for the most part, stopped asking God for things—and not due to some holy, saintly belief that I had all I need.

I would ask Him to bless my family, to protect Caroline, to give us wisdom as we raise her, but I had stopped asking for anything tangible because I was scared it wouldn't happen and I didn't want to be disappointed in God. I am embarrassed by my lack of faith, especially in light of how faithful God has always been to provide for all my needs and exceed my expectations in so many ways.

It began sometime after Caroline was born. I prayed so hard that I could stay home with her, and when maternity leave ended and no one had delivered a bag of money and health insurance to our front door, I was disappointed. I accepted it, but part of me didn't understand why it hadn't worked out the way I'd hoped.

So, in time, I tucked all my hopes and dreams in a little corner and kept them to myself. Honestly, I don't think I ever admitted to myself how frustrated I felt. Plus, a huge part of me recognized all the blessings in my life that I didn't really deserve, so why would I complain about what I didn't have?

I stopped asking God for the things that were most important to me. I let fear control me. Fear of letting go, fear of surrendering, fear of disappointment, fear of things not working out the way I wanted them to, fear of where He might lead me.

But then I began to realize that we chase after God's heart not by blandly accepting whatever comes our way but by opening our hearts with vulnerability, submission, and trust.

When you consider God's infinite wisdom and love for us, the fact that God tells us to ask Him for what we need is an invitation that we'd be stupid, in our own infinite shortsightedness, not to accept.

Let's trust His heart and ask Him for the things we want. He wants us to ask because He knows it's an important step of faith and helps us know Him more in all the different aspects of our life.

GOD DID THIS

···

By day the LORD went ahead of them in a pillar of cloud
to guide them on their way and by night in a pillar of
fire to give them light, so that they could travel by day
or night. Neither the pillar of cloud by day nor the pillar
of fire by night left its place in front of the people.

EXODUS 13:21-22

One of my favorite books is *The Middle Place* by Kelly Corrigan. It's a memoir about a young mom diagnosed with breast cancer. She realizes as she calls her parents with the news that she is in the middle place of her life, both a mother to her daughters and a child to her parents.

I think the story resonates so strongly with me because we live the bulk of our lives in the middle place. Beginnings are exciting. Even endings can be interesting because an ending usually signals completion or the end of a journey or even that you're about to have a new beginning. But it's the middle that usually defines who we are and who we'll become.

Like middle school and middle age, the middle can often be mundane, tedious, and even scary. The middle sometimes brings hard times, and we find ourselves anxiously yearning to get to the other side.

The children of Israel are such a clear portrait of the Middle Place.

They were slaves in Egypt when God raised up Moses as their leader. Even

Moses himself was in a middle place—Hebrew by birth and Egyptian by adoption. God called him to lead the children of Israel out of Egypt, and where did Moses lead them? To the middle of the desert.

The Bible tells us that God took the Israelites on the longer route on their journey to the Promised Land: "When Pharaoh let the people go, God did not lead them on the road through the Philistine country, though that was shorter. For God said, 'If they face war, they might change their minds and return to Egypt.' So God led the people around by the desert road toward the Red Sea" (Exodus 13:17–18).

God could have taken them straight from Pharaoh to Canaan, but what would the story be? What would the Israelites have learned? Would they have had the opportunity to witness His glory?

God wants to give us a story. Something we can look back on and say, "GOD DID THIS." And that story is found in the middle places between where we've been and where we're going, in the middle places of where we don't want to be and where His promises are revealed, in the middle places of difficult days and who God is shaping us to be.

The children of Israel found themselves in the middle, between a vast body of water and an approaching Egyptian army. And then Moses parted the Red Sea and led the Israelites through *the middle* of the waters. And it is here—between the familiar and the unknown—where the Hebrew people got the first real glimpse of who their God was and what He could do.

Right after this, Moses acknowledges how big God is—above and beyond what he has ever known and with him at all times—and he says, "Who among the gods is like you, LORD? Who is like you—majestic in holiness, awesome in glory, working wonders?" (15:11).

Moses most clearly saw God in the middle.

I'm learning that you can't rush through the middle because some things God can teach us only in the journey. And ultimately our entire lives are a journey. Beginning, middle, end. God alone sets the pace.

We have such a human tendency to rush to the next thing and the next thing because it might bring us fulfillment, might be the missing piece, might be what we've been waiting for to bring us peace. The next job, graduating from college, getting married, having our first baby, and then having our second baby—it's a cycle of the next thing. But growth and true intimacy with God comes in the middle places. And it's in developing intimacy with Him that we find joy.

It's in the middle that we often experience the heartbreak and hard times of life, but it's also those times when we see God for who He really is if we stop and look. When we realize we don't have the answers or the strength or the ability on our own, when our resources are all gone, we look to Him.

Best of all, He promises to go before us and meet us right there in the middle.

Day 14

MIRROR, MIRROR

··

May these words of my mouth and this meditation
of my heart be pleasing in your sight, LORD.

PSALM 19:14

Now that I actually make a living from writing (pro tip: This is a great career path for those of you who like a good reason to stay in your pajamas for days and lack social skills), I find that I edit my work constantly. I've realized that the words I choose can completely make or break a story. In fact, a few weeks ago I was reading a memoir by an author who used such graphic imagery that I had to actually walk away from it because it was too painful to read.

One of my favorite quotes about the use of words is by Anne Lamott: "You own everything that happened to you. Tell your stories. If people wanted you to write warmly about them, they should have behaved better." This is true—except we all know (or have learned the hard way) that there is fallout from the words we choose to say or not say. Which is why I've always claimed that my best book will be the one I write thirty years from now, entitled *Now That Everybody Is Dead*.

Proverbs 13:3 says, "Those who guard their lips guard their lives, but those who speaks rashly will come to ruin." *To ruin.* That's not exactly a small promise, like, "He'll really regret it." Our words have the power to ruin lives. It can be so easy to forget that in the heat of the moment. Jesus says, "What you say flows from what is in your heart" (Luke 6:45 NLT). Our words reveal what we really think or feel even when we don't mean for them to, and they always have some impact or consequence, even when we don't realize it. I have the tendency to always go for the funny, sarcastic comment, and I've had to learn over the years when it's better to keep my mouth shut than to go for the easy laugh that could end up hurting someone's feelings.

We have so many more ways to put our words out for public consumption . . . blogs, Twitter, Facebook, Instagram. And we've seen the words someone using being misconstrued or taken out of context (or just being foolish and shortsighted—and so damaging). I caution Caroline all the time that the internet is FOREVER and your true meaning can't always be understood in a quick text or email. We need to be so careful about how we use our words because relationships are built on words. Our lives are defined by our words. And the best way to ensure our words are kind is to fill our heart with the Word of God.

A while back, I attended an event with various booths and displays set up around the main conference room. One of the features was called the "I'm Enough" mirror. It was reminiscent of the mirror in *Snow White*, where you could gaze at your reflection while wearing headphones that spoke prerecorded affirmations in your ear like "You are beautiful," "You are talented," and "You are good enough, smart enough, and, doggone it, people like you." (I don't know if it really said that. Let me have my dream.) It struck me as the saddest thing I'd ever seen. Are we at a point where we need prerecorded affirmations to make us feel good?

I believe we are called to use our words to honor God and to bless those around us. Our words should refresh each other's souls and speak life and blessing. We need to lift up and encourage one another. Ultimately, this applies to the words we say to ourselves. Satan whispers that we are failures, that we aren't enough, that people would turn their backs on us if they knew who we really are. But when we read God's Word, we see that we are His portion and His prize, that He created us for a purpose and has plans to give us a hope and a future (Jeremiah 29:11).

Let's make these the words that overflow from our hearts and our mouths. Because no one should have to rely on a mirror and some headphones.

SIDE EFFECTS MAY INCLUDE . . .

> But David said to Saul, "Your servant has
> been keeping his father's sheep."
>
> **1 SAMUEL 17:34**

My first job after college was in financial sales. This may not seem disturbing until I tell you that I made a D in my only finance class in college. I apologize to anyone whose 401(k) is all jacked up thanks to my lack of basic investment knowledge. However, that job did teach me how to make an effective presentation, which led to a better job in pharmaceutical sales. And ultimately, both of those jobs, neither of which were my passion, ended up preparing me for the public speaking I do now. Apparently people assume that if you write books, you should also speak. The point is, God used those things in my life that seemed insignificant to prepare me for the ministry He has called me to, which makes me realize that God often teaches us the most important lessons and skills in obscurity.

When you look at the life of David, it was in the pasture, tending sheep, where David learned to be king, not on a throne. He learned how to lead and be tender. He learned responsibility, he learned how to be a provider and a protector, and he learned how to throw a stone. And most important, he sat in the quiet places with God and learned how big our God is and how deep His love.

David never forgot this lesson, and it's what made him a man after God's own heart. David knew how deeply he was loved, and that knowledge brought him to redemption and repentance every time he messed up. When we read the 23rd Psalm written by David, we can see how much he learned about who God is in the quiet pastures of his life.

> The LORD is my shepherd, I lack nothing. He makes me lie down in green pastures, he leads me beside quiet waters, he refreshes my soul. He guides me along the right paths for his name's sake. Even though I walk through the darkest valley, I will fear no evil, for you are with me; your rod and your staff, they comfort me.

A calling from God requires our cooperation to wait on His timing, knowing that God is teaching us and shaping us in preparation for the tasks He has ahead for us. We tend to emphasize the big because we have forgotten the value of the small. God sees our everyday tasks as sacred work. We are His hands and feet in this world. That smile you give to the grocery store cashier, that diaper you're changing, and that carpool you're driving? They all matter.

We have so many questions and so much confusion about God's will for our lives, but here's the thing: you are in God's will when you are doing all the things you do every day to serve the people around you. You are in God's will when you wake up in the morning with a heart that says you'll go where He leads today and ask to see Him in the ordinary.

Os Guiness says, "Grand Christian movement will rise and fall. Grand campaigns will be mounted and grand coalitions assembled. But all together such coordinated efforts will never match the influence and untold numbers of followers of Christ living out their callings faithfully across the vastness and complexity of modern society."

Little things add up to big things in God's economy.

Will we be faithful when no one is watching? Will we be faithful even when we don't feel like it? Because our feelings will come and go, but His love for us won't.

Just because I have days when I don't feel in love with my husband doesn't mean he ceases to exist or to be my provider and protector. How much truer is this with God?

It's in the quiet places where we can receive a fresh word and hear His voice. And it's a fresh word that keeps us from becoming self-righteous and believing we know all there is to know about ourselves and God and the world around us. His voice is our daily bread. The manna that sustains us. And just like manna, it is new every morning.

We are surrounded by distractions, but we need to take time to listen for God's voice. It's often the thing that gets drowned out. God sometimes speaks the loudest in the quietest, most seemingly insignificant places in our lives, and we'll learn from Him only when we remember that God uses every bit of our lives for His glory and His purposes. Never underestimate how He is using you while you're sitting in a cubicle or washing another load of dirty towels to make a difference.

THE ADVENTURE OF OPEN DOORS

....

Forgetting what is behind and straining toward what is
ahead, I press on toward the goal to win the prize for
which God has called me heavenward in Christ Jesus.

PHILIPPIANS 3:13–14

Sometimes I think back on my life and what I wish my eighteen-year-old self had known. What would I tell myself if I could go back?

Here are a few thoughts:

1. Buy some stock in Apple.
2. Don't take Japanese as your foreign language choice in college. You'll be shocked at how few occasions you'll have to compliment the people of Japan on their lovely cherry blossom trees.
3. Wear sunscreen.

But maybe most of all, I'd tell myself not to be so afraid of the future. Yes, life has come with its share of heartaches and hard times, but things have a way of working out in the long run. I've always been one to fight change with everything in me because it intimidates me to leave behind what is comfortable and familiar.

Yet I've realized that you won't get very far in life if you stick to what you already know and where you've already been. The only way to move forward is to actually take that step through the open door in front of you, and ultimately, there are no greater adventures in life than open doors. Like C. S. Lewis said, "There are far, far better things ahead than any we leave behind."

God won't call each of us to the same thing. Our lives will look as different as we are and as unique as the gifts God has given each of us. But a true call from God to move forward will bring us to a place of deeper dependence on Him. If your vision of what God has for you is something you feel totally capable of in your own power, then you're not seeing the whole picture. God will always call us higher and deeper than we can go on our own. And here's what I've discovered: no one in the Bible immediately responds with "I'M READY" when God calls. Instead, they often give a list of excuses as to why God should choose someone else.

Bible characters! They're just like us!

But it's our willingness to go through the open doors that we don't expect or feel prepared for that turns our lives into a great adventure and more than we could have imagined for ourselves.

If you open yourself up to the life God has for you, it probably won't look like you had planned . . . but it will be infinitely better because you will be living a life of purpose.

BUT BETTER

....

Every good and perfect gift is from above, coming
down from the Father of the heavenly lights,
who does not change like shifting shadows.

JAMES 1:17

On Mother's Day 2002, I was seven weeks pregnant. I was excited, hopeful, and giddy. Perry and I had prayed for a baby, and now one was on the way. I remember sitting in church that Sunday feeling so blessed to be on my way to becoming a baby-carrying, spit up-wearing member of the motherhood sorority.

And then two weeks later, we found ourselves sitting in the doctor's office as he told us there was no heartbeat, no baby.

I didn't know it then, but that moment prepared me more for what motherhood really involves than if I had carried that baby to term.

Motherhood is about both holding someone close and letting them go all at the same time. It's about loving someone more than you ever imagined possible, yet not being able to completely protect them from all the challenges they will face. It's about wanting to do the best job imaginable and raise fine, upstanding members of society, but spending years and years wondering if it's actually going to happen because you can't even figure out how to teach them to use the toilet.

It's about trust. Trusting that God knows you and knows this child He has given you. Knowing that my strengths are designed to cover her weaknesses.

Knowing that even before I was born, God knew He would someday entrust Caroline to me. It overwhelms me.

One afternoon, when Caroline was about four, a thunderstorm came through the city, and after it was over, an incredible rainbow appeared in the sky. I carried Caroline outside to see it and watched her face as she stared in pure amazement while my heart exploded just a little bit.

Then she declared, "Oh, Mama. It's just like in my books, but better!"

And I was thinking the same thing. *Motherhood is just what I dreamed about, but better.*

(Full disclosure: it's also messier and involves more throw up and peanut butter than I expected too.)

Day 18

YOUR FATHER LOVES YOU

....

"See, I have engraved you on the palms of my hands."

ISAIAH 49:16

Many years ago, I watched Steven Curtis Chapman and his family being interviewed on *Good Morning America* and *Larry King Live* after the tragic loss of their five-year-old daughter.

One thing that came up in both interviews that brought tears to my eyes was when Steven said someone later told him that as he was being driven to the hospital where his daughter had just been Life-Flighted, Steven rolled down the window and yelled to his devastated son, who had accidentally run over her, "Will Franklin! Your father loves you!"

What an incredible picture of how much a parent loves a child! That even in the midst of tragedy, Steven made sure his son knew that he was loved. But even more than that, I cried because, maybe for the first time, I realized that that is how God loves me. How many times have I been broken by my fears, my failures, my disappointments? How many times have I doubted, questioned, disappointed, and disobeyed him and wondered why things aren't working out the way I want them to?

God has whispered to my heart in all those times—both at my lowest points and at my highest points. He has looked at me and said, "Melanie! Your father loves you!"

This shouldn't have been a new revelation to me. But it was.

When I think back to my childhood, I don't remember hearing much about God's grace. I'm not saying it wasn't being taught; it just never really sunk in. Maybe I heard one too many flannel-board Sunday school stories about Sodom and Gomorrah.

Whatever the case, I have struggled with grasping God's mercy and grace. I struggle with how He can love me so much when I so often feel like I've failed. And at the heart of that is a trust issue. Do I trust that God's love is stronger than my failures? Can His grace cover my flaws? Do I trust that He wants to pour out blessings on me that I don't deserve and gives them anyway because that's how much He loves me?

After I watched that interview, I couldn't get the image out of my head that God sees me this way, that He feels this kind of love for me. That I am His child and He longs to hold me close the same way I long to hold Caroline close and cherish every single ounce of her, but even more so.

I've read Psalm 139 countless times. I know He knows my thoughts, I know He knows my words before they are on my tongue, I know He knows the numbers of hairs on my head (which are grayer than they used to be), and I know His thoughts of me outnumber the grains of sand. I know it because I've heard it all my life. But in the days following the Chapman interview, I felt like He began to really *reveal* to me the depths of His love. Not for all humankind, not for every bit of creation—but specifically *for me*.

At church the following Sunday, I was standing during praise and worship, and I felt God say to me, "I know your name. I know everything about you, and I adore you. No matter what." It's like I could hear Him saying my name. My full name, over and over again. *Melanie. Melanie. Melanie.* Just as I was feeling that in my heart, our pastor began to speak. Guess what he said? "God knows your name. He knows everything about you."

Is it just me or do you think God was trying to tell me something?

God's love for the world isn't general. It's not merely an all-encompassing "I love My creation" thing. It's *specific*. Specifically for me. Specifically for you.

In spite of who we are, in spite of how we fail, in spite of all our weaknesses.

Because here's the thing: He made us. He knows us. None of our shortcomings or moral failures surprise Him. God doesn't sit in heaven saying, "Wow. I did *not* see that coming."

He sits in heaven with a deep longing to take us in His arms, spin us around, and say "Melanie! Your Father loves you!"

Except He would call you by your name, not mine. Because He's God.

And He knows your name.

DON'T STOP ASKING

"Until now you have not asked for anything in my name.
Ask and you will receive, and your joy will be complete."

JOHN 16:24

I subscribe to a service that delivers a daily Bible verse straight to your email inbox every morning. We live in a glorious era, when virtually anything can be delivered straight to our front door or our email. I have to say: it's a great time to be alive. The email Bible verse of the day is a good system for me because I'm not always the best about opening my Bible to start the day. This ensures that I at least begin my day with a little bit of scripture. Last week, I began to notice that *every* day, the verse of the day was about asking anything of God and receiving it. On Saturday morning, when yet another verse rolled in about asking God and having faith, I turned around and laughingly told Perry, "I think God is telling me to ask Him for something." Perry agreed that my superb powers of intuition were probably right. It only took me a week to catch on. God was probably sitting in heaven thinking He should have made me a little quicker on my feet.

I immediately thought through all the potential things I could ask of God. We are in a new season of life right now as Caroline is getting older, and there is so much to ask for: financial provision, health, peace, contentment. The world around us feels a little darker and scarier than normal. I could come up with a veritable laundry list of potential requests.

Then, yesterday morning, I checked the verse of the day. It was Mark 11:24: "Therefore, I tell you, whatever you ask for in prayer, believe that you have received it, and it will be yours." It was the seventh straight day that was about asking God for something in prayer. I can honestly say that I didn't even know there were so many verses about asking for things.

I finally realized that the reason God kept tugging at my heart and giving me sign after sign to ask Him for something is because I have basically stopped asking Him for things. And not due to some holy, saintly belief that I have all I need. I'll ask Him to bless my family, to protect Caroline, to give us wisdom as we raise her, but I've quit asking for anything tangible because I am scared it won't happen—and I don't want to be disappointed in God. Even as I type that, I am embarrassed by my lack of faith, especially in light of how faithful God has always been to provide for all my needs and exceed my expectations in so many ways.

Over time, I've slowly stopped asking God for the things that are most important to me. I have been letting fear control me. Fear of letting go, fear of surrendering, fear of disappointment, fear of things not working out the way I want them to, fear of where He may lead. And now He's telling me I have to let go and just *ask*. Yes, sometimes the answer may not be what I want and sometimes there will be answers I don't understand, but ultimately I have to trust in Ephesians 3:20: "Now to him who is able to do immeasurably more than all we ask or imagine, according to his power that is at work within us." I have watched over the last year as God has done more than I could ask or imagine. Despite my unwillingness to ask Him for the desires of my heart, He has searched the corners of my heart and answered so many hidden requests. And it's a reminder to me never to be afraid to ask for what I want.

LOST AND FOUND

And my God will meet all your needs according
to his glorious riches in Christ Jesus.

PHILIPPIANS 4:19

One morning, Perry got up exceptionally early and headed down to the ranch in South Texas where he hunts. When Caroline and I woke up later that morning, I walked by the back door and noticed our dogs weren't on the back porch. I didn't think anything of it because, first of all, I don't think about anything that early in the morning, and, secondly, I assumed Perry had taken them with him to the ranch because he usually does. I should also tell you that this was years ago, when we had our dogs Scout and Bruiser. They have since gone to meet Jesus.

Perry called about forty-five minutes after we were awake to see how our morning was going. I told him it was the usual and then I casually said, "I assume you have the dogs with you."

"I don't have the dogs. Are they not in the backyard?"

"Umm, I don't think so . . ."

I ran out on the back porch and started calling the dogs.

Nothing. No dogs in the backyard.

Caroline was following me and was beside herself at the drama that was playing out right before her very eyes. Finally, Scout came walking up from the other side of the yard, but Bruiser was nowhere to be found. I informed Perry that Bruiser was missing, and we realized he must have gotten out when Perry's employees came by earlier to pick up some equipment.

I hurried to finish getting Caroline dressed and ready, and since we still had some time before school started, I drove around the neighborhood while Caroline and I both yelled, "BRUISER! BRUISER!" But he was nowhere to be found. As I walked Caroline to her classroom, she looked up at me and said, "Mama, *why* would Bruiser want to leave our family?" We said a prayer that Bruiser would come home, and I kissed her goodbye and left to go look for the dog.

I spent hours driving, walking all over our neighborhood, calling for Bruiser. Perry pulled his guys off the job site so they could drive around and look, and he headed home from the ranch to join the search

No Bruiser.

Finally, it was time to pick up Caroline from school, and as soon as I walked in the door, her teacher asked if I'd found our dog because it was all Caroline had talked about. In fact, she was even stopping people in the hallway to tell them our tale of pet loss woe and had asked for prayer for Bruiser in chapel. I told the teacher that we hadn't found Bruiser, and she gave me a look that conveyed the mental calculations she was doing of the years of therapy Caroline would require due to all the pet negligence in our home.

On the way home, I explained to Caroline that it was really hot and Bruiser was probably just resting somewhere and would come home later on. Perry had come home and had to get something out of our back house. He opened the door and discovered that I was right: Bruiser was resting. In our back house. Where he'd been the entire time.

But I wasn't the only one who had been looking for our sleeping dog.

Perry had two guys working for him back in those days, Gus and Shorty. Normally Gus runs his own business, but he had been helping Perry out for the last week, so he and Shorty had just met. Gus is an awesome Christian man. He's one of those people that exudes kindness and gentleness from every pore, and if you spend two seconds with him, he'll tell that you the source of all his joy and happiness is his faith in Jesus.

Shorty is a little bit of a rough character. I don't even know his whole story, but I know that life has been hard. He's done a lot of really rough living and always seems a little beaten down.

On the day Bruiser went missing, Gus and Shorty spent four hours together, just the two of them, riding around in Gus's truck, looking for Bruiser. Gus told Perry later that while Shorty thought he was just looking for a dog, Gus showed him that he was looking for something else. Hope. Joy. Peace.

Gus talked to Shorty about God, about the hope found in Jesus, and Shorty listened. He really listened. And when Perry apologized to Gus for sending them on a mission to look for a dog that wasn't even lost, Gus told him it didn't matter because God used that time to make sure that Shorty was found.

Earlier that day, I had told Caroline to pray that we'd find Bruiser. I prayed that we'd find Bruiser—but I kind of threw it out there like it was a silly, frivolous thing to pray for. In the scale of big happenings and tragedies, a lost dog doesn't really rank that high. But in light of how the events of the day unfolded, I realized that I'm doubting God's authority and power over *every* area of life. I often have Him reserved to handle the really big things but don't give Him a lot of the day-to-day things.

And look what He did. He used a non-lost dog to save a lost man.

Now that's creative.

UNLIKELY WARRIORS

When the angel of the LORD appeared to Gideon,
he said, "The LORD is with you, mighty warrior."

JUDGES 6:12

I've had times in my life when I've just felt stagnant, kind of like I knew where life was headed . . . but then it seems to stall out a little or take me in a different direction that I don't necessarily want to go. And the truth is that sometimes I just get tired and lose my way.

I was reading through Judges the other day and came to the story of Gideon in chapter 6. The Israelites have been invaded by the Midianites and are totally oppressed by them. In the midst of all this is a man named Gideon who is threshing wheat in a winepress. Normally, according to my vast and nonexistent wheat-threshing expertise, he'd thresh his wheat out in the open. But Gideon was afraid of the Midianites and was hiding in a winepress.

So while Gideon was hiding out, an angel appeared to him and said, "The LORD is with you, mighty warrior." Oh, how I *love* an angel who deals in irony. Mighty warrior? Gideon is hiding! He's threshing his wheat in fear, and yet the angel calls him a mighty warrior.

The angel has come to tell Gideon that God is going to use him to deliver the Israelites from Midian. At first Gideon doesn't believe it. In fact, he asks God for a sign two different times to make sure he's heard God right. Ultimately Gideon ends up being exactly what the angel called him—a mighty warrior. He defeats the Midianites using only three hundred men. Do you see what God did there? He called Gideon to something he never could have imagined for himself. That's what God does.

God sees what we can't see. He sees something where there is nothing. And even though I've read the story of Gideon and had that revelation before, I saw it with fresh eyes the other day. I needed the reminder that God sees something in me that I don't see in myself. I see all my fears and insecurities and worries and just general yuck, but He looks at me and sees something entirely different. He sees something He can use for His plans and purposes.

Honestly, I don't really know what that looks like right now. This has been a year of God changing my heart about some things and keeping my heart hoping for others. It's been a year of me wanting to know all the answers but at the same time realizing that knowing all the answers doesn't require faith.

All that to say, I want to listen for His voice and see more of what He sees because He knows to look at the part of us where we see nothing and He sees a mighty warrior.

ROOTED IN HIM

In him was life, and that life was the light of
all mankind. The light shines in the darkness,
and the darkness has not overcome it.

JOHN 1:4–5

Perry and I moved into our house six months after we got married. We were just two skinny newlyweds back then, and when our realtor showed us this little cottage house that was the only semi-decent thing in our price range (and by *semi-decent*, I mean the only one without shag carpet left over from the seventies), we signed the contract and became real grownups in the form of a thirty-year mortgage, the way God and the Bank of America intended.

We saw promise in this house that was painted a hideous shade of yellow with mint green trim. And that was before mint green had made a comeback. Seriously, mint green is everywhere right now. I don't totally understand it, but it's better than jelly shoes and ribbon belts, so let's just go with it.

Perry was in full-time ministry at the time but now owns a landscaping business. And I guess his landscaper's eye made it our top priority to get rid of the hideous, overgrown ligustrums on the west side of the house and replace them with two beautiful mountain laurel trees. In case you don't know, few things are better than a mountain laurel in spring. They get these gorgeous lavender blossoms that smell like grape soda and basically make the world feel like a better place.

So we had a company come plant our trees. The next spring, they were covered in blooms, and we declared them worth every penny. We had tree pride and were sure all our neighbors had tree envy. (Not really. I don't think tree envy is a real thing. Unless maybe you're a botanist.)

But over the ensuing years, they quit producing as many blooms. They began to look a little pitiful. I mean, they were still alive, but I'd drive around town and see other trees that had flowers all over them and I'd feel bad about my trees. Maybe tree envy *is* a real thing and I had it.

Finally, last spring, Perry had a tree specialist come out and look at our trees to see if we had a problem. The tree guy took one look at them and immediately made his diagnosis. When the trees were initially planted, they were planted too deep. Over the years, the roots had become covered by more and more layers of dirt and mulch until they weren't getting enough light from above.

Hi. Spiritual analogy, anyone?

The tree guy brought in some kind of equipment that I'd tell you all about except I didn't care enough to ask, and he dug out all the excess dirt around the tree roots to expose them to the light. And I am not kidding when I tell you that not even two weeks later, both of our trees were covered in the bright green foliage that's a sign of new growth and health. That's all it took. The roots needed light.

Those trees have been a reminder to me that I let too many things crowd in and block out the voice of God in my life. And not even bad things necessarily, just busy things. It's hard to balance all the carpooling and cooking chicken for dinner and acting as the cruise director for our family. These are all good (well, maybe not the chicken), yet they can add to the busyness that distracts me from absorbing how much God loves me.

I struggle with grace. I struggle to comprehend that I am fully loved by God no matter how much I fail. That's the place I go when I let too much dirt cover up the truth of God in my life.

Because I know myself. I know all my weaknesses and failures. I know what I've done and what I regret and what I've been saved from. I know all the ways I continue to fail on a daily basis. And if I'm disappointed in myself, how is *God* not disappointed in me? How does He look at me with unfailing love and hope that I'll do better tomorrow . . . and yet won't love me any less if I don't? It doesn't make sense. And sometimes it just feels easier to cover these insecurities up and pretend they're not there instead of exposing them to the light.

Over the last few weeks, God has shown His love to me in a hundred different ways, small, simple things. Some moments I've almost felt like it was too much, more than I deserve. And I've felt Him say to me in the deepest part of my heart, the part I sometimes let get too covered up, "You are so much harder on yourself than I am."

He's right. I'm hard on myself. I get caught up in the comparison game and feel like everyone is loving better, living more purposefully, doing more significant things, and essentially, blooming so much better than me. I give other people the benefit of the doubt, but I never give myself that same grace. And that's what God has been whispering over me.

Grace.

I don't know if any of us have the capability or the comprehension to ever fully grasp the love of God. It's too big. But I know that the only way we'll ever grow and become what He has called us to be is when we expose ourselves to the light. That's where we bloom. And that's where we find ourselves immersed in the fragrance that tells the world who we belong to, what He has done for us, and that we are covered in ridiculous amounts of grace by the light of His truth.

Day 23

#BLESSED

Am I now trying to win the approval of men, or of
God? Or am I trying to please men? If I were still trying
to please men, I would not be a servant of Christ.

GALATIANS 1:10

I have a confession: I am a people pleaser. I want people to like me. I want everyone to think I'm nice. Misunderstandings make me cringe, and controversy makes me want to run and hide. When I was growing up, my parents got divorced and we stopped going to the Catholic church and began attending a wild, fully Pentecostal church that met in a double-wide trailer. I remember longing to be a nice, normal Episcopalian like all the other kids at school. I like to blend in and not open myself up in a way that may cause people to say, "Well, *that's* weird."

And now that I have a daughter in junior high, I sometimes find myself worrying if we are doing the right things. Is she making friends? Should we try harder to be a part of this group or that group? Do we have to join a service club just because everyone else is?

We live in a world where approval matters. Just look at social media. Twitter, Instagram, and Facebook are all geared around getting likes or having people tell us we're winning at life. We want our homes to be beautiful, our kids to be on the honor roll, and our marriages to be awesome. In short, we want to appear to be #blessed.

The problem is that we will always have critics. One of my favorite Twitter accounts is Amazon movie reviews. It's proof that people will find a way to criticize anything. A one-star review for *How to Train Your Dragon* stated, "The aerodynamics in this movie are not very realistic. Also, that's not what dragons looks like," and a one-star review for *Pretty Woman* said, "They have a lot of nerve naming this movie *Pretty Woman* and should be ashamed of themselves. Julia Roberts's mouth is way too big. A person's mouth should not go more than halfway around their head." Well. That seems harsh.

Sometimes our loudest critics are our own family members. We were never smart enough or athletic enough. We should have been doctors. We can spend our entire lives trying to please our critics, and ultimately they will never be satisfied. There is always something else to criticize.

Which is why I need to remember that the only approval that matters is God's. Nobody knows you like God knows you. You can't know someone's marriage or life unless you've lived it. We're all good at putting on a brave face and acting like everything is okay even when we're hurting inside. And since only God knows us inside and out, His approval is what matters.

What will make us stand out in this world is *looking* different. Our relationships should look different; our kids should be raised to love Christ and put Him first; we need to lay down what we want for what Christ wants. That's the key to living life with the security that can only come from God—because when our security comes from knowing who we are in Christ and what He has done for us, others' opinions matter less. And we realize we are so very loved.

I encourage you to find the purpose for which you were created and quit worrying what others think. Because when we're doing what God created us to do, we'll find fulfillment that no worldly approval can offer. We become secure in the choices we make for ourselves in our marriages, with our children, and in our careers, knowing that we have the approval of the only One who matters, the only One we'll stand in front of at the end of our lives and from whom we hope to hear "Well done."

Day 24

HOW TO BE BRAVE

God has not given us a spirit of fear, but of
power and of love and of a sound mind.

2 TIMOTHY 1:7 NKJV

A few months ago, I was in the grocery store doing my normal grocery shopping when my phone rang. I reached into my purse and answered. It was my gynecologist's office, and, well, I'm at a point in my life that when my gynecologist calls, I listen. And now I need to quit talking about this. Forever.

The nurse on the other end verified that it was me and then said, "I'm calling because the imaging service found something suspicious on the mammogram you had last week." And just like that, I left my cart in the middle of the frozen foods aisle and walked out of the store, because I was gripped by fear and certain I was dying and because who needs groceries when you have cancer?

I'd just watched one of my oldest, dearest friends lose a five-year battle with breast cancer and had a front-row seat to the devastation, so this pronouncement from the nurse sent me into a bit of an amplified fear spiral. All I could think as I hung up was that it felt appropriate that I was trying to decide whether to buy ice cream when all the pieces of my world felt like they might crash down.

The truth is, we live in a broken world where really bad things can and do happen. Fear exists because most of us have lived long enough to know that life can throw us curve balls. But how much we ultimately fear is an indicator of our faith.

For me, when I let fear overwhelm me, I find that I start trying to control everything I possibly can. If I read a tragic story online, I attempt to manage my fear by believing I can control the events that caused that bad thing to happen. Was he wearing a helmet? Did they let their kids walk to school alone? Did they wear sunscreen? Maybe they drank too many Diet Cokes. It's a dumb game I play in my head in a sad attempt to control my fear. But what if I could trust God enough to surrender whatever illusion of control I think I have and just say, "I trust You. I trust Your heart. I trust Your plan for my life and the lives of everyone I love"?

I read once that faith isn't the absence of fear. Faith is being afraid of doing something—and then doing it anyway. It's letting go of our kids, our finances, our marriage, and saying, "Here You go, God. I trust You with all of this."

We are a generation of parents who would put our kids in one enormous bike helmet if we could. But here's the thing: I don't want to raise a scared kid. Because you know what scared kids don't do? They don't grow up to be people who can impact their world. I don't want to raise a precious snowflake. I want to raise a fearless world-changer who bravely goes where God calls.

And the best way to do that is to show our kids what it looks like to be brave. They need to see us step out and face the scary thing. They need to see us trust God with the hard things. We need to let them try new things, let them succeed, and let them fail. Only God knows the plans He has for our lives, and we need to trust Him and stop living in fear of all the what-ifs. The what-ifs rarely happen, and even if they do, we are incapable of fathoming the grace and love God will give us as we walk down that hard road. He always goes before us.

Last spring, I watched a mama bird build a nest in the wreath on our front door. She tirelessly lined it with feathers and twigs and other treasures she'd found in the neighborhood, and then she laid her eggs. When the eggs hatched, we loved watching those baby birds as they waited for their mama to return with whatever food she'd found for them. That mama bird did her best to create a safe home for her babies, but there was no way for her to know that it was nestled in our front door and that no matter how much we tried not to disturb them, we still had to use the front door on occasion. Those babies weren't entirely safe there, but she did her best to protect them and provide for them.

It reminded me of us. We do our best to build safe spaces in our lives and keep everyone warm and dry and fed, but because there are always outside factors beyond our control, ultimately it's all in God's hands.

And that's life. Situations and events will always be outside what we control and understand. And that's the point. God wants us in a place of trusting Him to provide and to protect. We were never meant to carry that burden alone.

As it turns out, my follow-up mammogram showed that there was nothing to be worried about. I had spent a week thinking through all the scenarios, usually envisioning the worst, for no reason. It made me think about dwelling on God's truth. Am I letting my imagination get away from me, or am I focusing on what I *know* to be true?

We could spend our entire lives worrying about cancer and all manner of scary things and miss out on what God has for us. Or we could learn to trust Him more and remember that He didn't create us to have a spirit of fear but of power and of love and of a sound mind.

THE BIGGER PERSON

Then I heard the voice of the LORD saying, "Whom shall I send?
And who will go for us?" And I said, "Here am I. Send me!"

ISAIAH 6:8

The last few months have been filled with a few situations that have made me feel left out. Nothing huge or earth-shattering by any stretch of the imagination, but enough to make me feel a little bit like I'm in fourth grade again and the last one picked for the kickball team—even though this is different because it's been years since I've kicked a big red ball *straight* back to the pitcher, making myself what is known as an easy out.

(Which only actually happened *twice*, by the way. Fourth-graders are an unforgiving bunch where kickball is concerned! And *whatever*. Some of us have different strengths.)

Honestly, I'd like to pretend like I am way too secure and confident to ever feel left out. I'd like to say that I'm a bigger person than that. But apparently I'm not. My best friend, Gulley, and I have this theory that sometimes the hardest thing about being the bigger person in a situation is that no one ever tells you you're being the bigger person. Which is why we now always make a point to tell each other when we think the other one is being a bigger person. We've had several conversations that end with one of us saying, "*Well*, let me assure you that *you* are the bigger person."

Which really has nothing to do with any of this but should rather be viewed as a side note providing full access into the way our minds work.

Anyway, the thing about feeling left out is that it turns into some sort of quicksand of self-doubt. *What's wrong with me? Am I not a likable person? Is it because I'm socially awkward? Am I not good enough? Is it because I admit to watching every season of* The Bachelor? *Do people think I'm shallow?*

Then I catch a glimpse of myself in the mirror and lose my train of thought because I notice a new gray hair, which leads to a full evaluation regarding the state of my eyebrows. There's no way anyone could think I'm shallow.

Basically I've been struggling with all these feelings of being inadequate and questioning why things happen the way they do and wondering why I'm not good enough for this or that.

The other night, I got in bed and couldn't sleep. I tossed and turned and eventually just decided to get still and hope that sleep would win out at some point. But my mind started racing with all these things I've perceived as slights, and I began to get worked up. All my doubts and fears came flying to the surface until I felt like I wanted to cry.

And at that moment, I felt God speak to my heart and say, "You need to quit asking Me 'Why?' and start asking Me 'Where?'"

I knew immediately that it was God's voice because I never would have come up with something that profound. And I certainly wouldn't have come up with something that succinct.

I've been in a cycle of asking "Why not me?" or "Why me?" or "Why is this so hard?" It's time for me to ask "Where would You have me go? Where would You have me serve? Where are You leading me?"

Don't get me wrong. I think there is a time to ask why. I have friends who are facing difficult circumstances, the kinds of things that can only leave a person to question why. And I think God understands that, even if we don't find the answer.

But my "Why?" had become a question that had me spiraling into a pit of self-pity. Which is hard to admit because I'd like to think I'm better than that.

See? I want to be the bigger person. LET ME BE THE BIGGER PERSON.

Asking "Where?" changes things though. It takes the focus off me and what I perceive to be my failures and shortcomings and puts the focus where it belongs: on God, the One who has plans and purposes for me despite my failures and fears. He knows what they are because He made me this way. And when I look to see where He's leading, I'm too busy following to spend a lot of useless time asking why.

Because the why doesn't really matter as much as the where.

The where is the question that asks, "What am I supposed to be doing?" instead of the why, which seems to say, "What am I doing wrong?"

I wish I could tie this all up and say I know exactly where I'm headed and what God has in store for me—or for you. But I don't. I don't know any of that right now. But I do know that it's about asking the right questions. It's not about us. It's about Him.

Day 26

SINKING IN GRACE

....

"My grace is sufficient for you, for my power is made perfect
in weakness." Therefore, I will boast all the more gladly about
my weaknesses, so that Christ's power may rest on me.

2 CORINTHIANS 12:9

The other day, I had almost two hours of uninterrupted car time. It's a rare thing these days to be in the car by myself, and I was thoroughly enjoying singing loudly and badly with no one to criticize me or ask if I'd please play "You Belong with Me" for the sixteenth time in a row.

As I settled in to the drive, I began to think about a lot of things. I am an optimist at heart and have never been one to live in gloom and doom for long. Because you know what has never solved a problem in the history of the world? Whining and complaining. It's true. Otherwise I could have solved a lot of problems in the early- to mid-nineties.

But I had a lot on my mind, specifically all the ways I felt like I was failing at life, marriage, motherhood, and making sure my family didn't run out of toilet paper. I was beating myself up about all the ways I needed to be better.

And it made me think of something I heard Beth Moore say one time: "We will never be secure until we realize we are fully loved by God, no matter our failings." That's it for me. I struggle with grace. I struggle to comprehend that I am fully loved by God no matter how much I fail.

Because I know myself. I *know* all my weaknesses and failures. I know what I've done and what I regret and what I've been saved from. I know all the ways I continue to fail on a daily basis. And if I'm disappointed in myself, how is *God* not disappointed in me? How does He look at me with unfailing love and hope that I'll do better tomorrow . . . but He won't love me any less if I don't?

It doesn't make sense.

As I drove, I started to think about the places I've been in life and how He's seen me through each and every one, confirmation that He was weaving together plans and purposes and a future that I couldn't have imagined.

I get caught up in the comparison game and feel like everyone is loving better, living more purposefully, doing more significant things, and has a better heart than I do. I give other people the benefit of the doubt, but I never give myself that same grace. And that's what God spoke to me yesterday. Grace.

He has never once looked at me, or you, shook His head, and said, "WOW. What a failure. I should have gotten someone else to do that." That's not how God works.

I don't know if any of us has the ability to ever fully grasp the love of God. It's too big. It defies all human rules and understanding. His grace is never-ending and is like the beams of the cross itself, higher than the heavens and as far as the east is from the west.

And it makes me think that maybe it's better to sink into God's grace rather than to try to keep swimming in my own power.

Day 27

HIS STARS

··

When I consider your heavens, the work of your fingers,
the moon and the stars, which you have set in place,
what is mankind that you are mindful of them?

PSALM 8:3–4

We have a fire pit in our backyard, and one of our favorite things to do as a family is to sit around the fire and look at the stars on a winter night. There's just something about the crisp winter air that makes it seem like everything in the night sky is shining just a little bit brighter.

Last year I even downloaded an app that allows you to hold your phone up to the sky to identify various constellations. I have to confess it hasn't really helped much. I still tend to be able to identify only the Big Dipper. Or maybe it's the Little Dipper. Or maybe it's Orion's Belt. I don't know. Quit bothering me. I am not an astronomer.

One night we read that Venus was going to be close enough to Earth to be seen with the naked eye, and sure enough, even a bunch of amateurs like us could see Venus just hanging out a few million miles away from the moon. (Or billion? Again. Not an astronomer.) All the stars that night seemed so bright. My husband, Perry, just happens to have night vision equipment, so he brought out his night vision goggles and we all took turns looking at the sky with the benefit of a device that allowed us to see more than we could have imagined.

All of a sudden, instead of just a smattering of stars, I realized the entire sky was *full* of stars you would never see just by looking up on a clear night with the naked eye. It was a symphony of light and movement.

And it made me think about our God who placed each of those stars—too many to count, stars yet to be discovered, stars that have shone for millions of years, and stars whose light burned out long ago. Yet He knows them all because He put them there. He is so vast, so powerful, so omnipresent. He is before all things and He holds every single bit of the universe in His hands.

Yet He chose *us*—humans. He could have stuck to creating stars. Surely they'd give Him a lot less trouble than we do. But He created all these things, *and then He created us.* Not because He had to but because of love.

And just like He holds all those stars in the night sky, He holds every detail of our lives in His hands.

FIGHTING OUR REFLECTION

The Lord will fight for you; you need only to be still.

EXODUS 14:14

I got my car washed a few days ago and was inordinately pleased with myself. A clean car makes me feel like a responsible adult. I may have let my family run out of toilet paper, but look at my clean car!

So I was irritated when I got to my car a few hours later and noticed bird poop down the driver's side door and little smeared scratch marks all over the side mirror. I wiped it clean with a damp paper towel, but the same thing happened the next day.

Later that afternoon, I was looking out my kitchen window and I saw the culprit: a little finch perched on the edge of my car door, fighting himself in my side mirror. He'd ruffle his feathers and swoop down at his image and then proceed to peck his reflection over and over again. He was repeating this process every single day, and as much as it made me laugh, it feels like there's a spiritual lesson in there somewhere.

We all have times in our life when we feel threatened and afraid. Maybe someone has hurt our family or someone we trusted let us down. Maybe the world at large just seems scary. Our instinct in these times is often to fight. Fight for control, fight to protect the ones we love, fight for self-preservation. Surely we can't just stand around and let it happen! We have to come out swinging.

But sometimes that fighting is as silly and pointless as that little finch fighting himself in my side mirror. We don't even know what we're fighting against or who the real enemy is, so we just peck and flutter around in a frenzy without accomplishing much beyond wearing ourselves out.

Meanwhile, we have a Father in heaven who promises to fight for us. He sees the entire picture, while we see only what we perceive to be the problem. Ultimately, the best thing we can do is to call on Him to fight our battles and learn to be still and trust that He is working all things together for our good. He is our defender; He is our strong tower; He is our mighty God.

And I don't know about you, but I find comfort and security in knowing that God fights our battles—the ones we are aware of and the ones we never see coming. That fact should allow our souls to rest and to stop fighting enemies that sometimes aren't even real.

Day 29

THE LIGHT OF
THE WORLD

....

"You are the light of the world. A town
built on a hill cannot be hidden."

MATTHEW 5:14

A while back, a high school student in our community committed suicide. In the days following, I watched people grapple with what should or could have been done differently and how to keep our kids from being bullied or being bullies themselves. Spoiler alert: I don't know all the answers.

But here are a few things I do know. I know that the darkness wants our kids. I know that evil is everywhere and is looking for a chance to whisper to them that they are less than, that they're inadequate, that they'll never be enough, and that their lives don't matter. I know that bullying has gone on since the beginning and has never been easier now that we can hide behind a keyboard and show our rear end without showing our face. I know that many people are more fragile than they appear and we need to treat our fellow human beings with kindness and respect even when they are different from us or we don't agree with them. And I know our kids are looking to us to model appropriate behavior. They may not act like it, but they know better than anyone if who we appear to be is the same person we are inside the walls of our home.

What if we teach our kids that their true identity and security is found in Christ? Each of us is wonderfully and fearfully made, and God has put us in our families, schools, communities, and world for a very specific and unique reason. And rather than finding power or making ourselves feel better by making someone else feel small, why not choose to be empowered by running *our own race*, to discover the purpose for which God has created us?

What if we showed our kids what kindness and compassion look like? It's never weak to show mercy and grace. Those characteristics are the very heartbeat of God. Let's live in a way that teaches our children the importance of loving our neighbors and that peers aren't our competition. We can cheer each other on without being afraid when we realize that God has each of us exactly where we're meant to be. The comparison trap is an endless vortex of nothingness that only serves to make us feel insecure and discontent because we are measuring our insides against someone else's outside.

God doesn't want us to live in fear. We can call on His power and love to stand up to the bullies and, maybe even more important, speak up for those who have been hurt too badly to defend themselves. A famous quote by Edmund Burke says, "The only thing necessary for the triumph of evil is for good men to do nothing." Let's raise good humans who aren't afraid to speak up or do something when they see wrong.

The thought that keeps running through my mind and heart is that we are called to be the light of the world, a city on a hill. In the days when Jesus spoke those words, a city lit up on a hill would have been a haven for weary travelers, a welcome sight that they were nearing a place where they could find a warm bed and a good meal. And the only way I know to accomplish that is to allow the love of Christ to take hold of our hearts and the hearts of our children so that we can show each other how to find a way home when we are lost, to hold out hope when we see someone is hurting, and that our differences only cause each of us to reflect our own unique ray of light in the midst of a dark night.

Day 30

GOD-GIVEN MOUTH

....

Moses said to the LORD, "Pardon your servant, Lord. I have never been eloquent, neither in the past nor since you have spoken to your servant. I am slow of speech and tongue." The LORD said to him, "Who gave human beings their mouths? Who makes them deaf or mute? Who gives them sight or makes them blind? Is it not I, the Lord? Now go; I will help you speak and will teach you what to say."

EXODUS 4:10–12

I am in the process of recovering from a bout of the flu. And by *process*, I mean that I am still finding it difficult to muster the strength to get out of my pajamas, and I have a lingering cough that would make a person with typhoid feel like they should avoid me, lest they *really* get sick.

The problem is that life is still happening, and so I've been forced to get up off my couch and engage in the real world. A trip to the grocery store yesterday proved that my seven days of isolation and illness have taken a toll on my social skills. I saw an acquaintance, and it was all I could do to make polite conversation because it felt like it took so much effort.

And it made me think about how often I say something I wish I hadn't said or the times I lie awake at night worrying that I said the wrong thing and inadvertently offended or hurt someone. We all have those situations where we just can't find the words or where the words we do come up with end up seeming totally insufficient or, worse, totally wrong.

A few weeks ago, a dear friend texted to let me know that her mother was in the final stages of her battle with cancer. I sat there with my phone in my hand until I finally texted back my honest response: "I don't know what to say. There are no words."

Maybe that's why I relate to this passage where Moses reminds God that he is totally ill-equipped for what he is being called to say. Convincing Pharaoh to let the children of Israel walk free definitely feels like something that would require a skilled orator who could make a persuasive case.

But God doesn't look at those things. He puts people and situations in our path, knowing that we are not equipped to deal with them on our own. It is only when we realize that God alone can give us what we need in any situation that we have the strength to get through it and to find the needed words. And I think it's so revealing that God specifically told Moses that he would "teach" him what to say. He didn't respond, "Oh, come ON, Moses. You know how to do this."

God gets it.

He gets our insufficiency, our insecurities, our fear of saying or doing the wrong thing. And He reminds us not only that He is the one who made our mouths in the first place but that He promises to teach us how to say the words that need to be said.

Day 31

LET YOUR LIGHT SHINE BRIGHT

···

For you were once darkness, but now you are light in
the Lord. Live as children of light for the fruit of the light
consists in all goodness, righteousness and truth.

EPHESIANS 5:8–9

I drive Caroline to school most mornings, and we always pray for her day. And then as she gets out of the car, I almost always remind her to "Let your light shine bright!" This is sometimes met with a smile and occasionally with an eye roll, depending on her mood. It's just my reminder that we are always called to be a light in the world and that some of the kids who walk the halls of her school desperately need to see a little light.

When Clemson won the National Championship, their coach, Dabo Swinney, told reporters after the game that he just kept encouraging his players to "let the light inside of them shine brighter than the light that was on them." I love that. Because it's the light of Christ inside us—never a spotlight on ourselves—that makes a difference in the world.

Part of the reason I encourage Caroline to let her light shine bright is because it reminds me that I need to do the same. Where can I help? How can I encourage someone going through a hard time? Who can I reach out to with a kind word?

Because I remember what it feels like to walk in darkness and fear and loneliness. I know that feeling of hearing a voice tell you you're not good enough or valuable or that your life doesn't mean much.

But that's where Jesus comes in. He *is* the light. And He shines His light in us and on us, and it's up to us to be the light in our little corner of the world.

So make the phone call. Send that text. Smile at that stranger. Speak a kind word.

Let your light shine bright.

Day 32

THE POWER OF
SMALL ACTS

....

"'Well done, good and faithful servant! You have been
faithful with a few things; I will put you in charge of many
things. Come and share your master's happiness!'"

MATTHEW 25:21

In the parable of the master and the bags of gold, we see three different scenarios. The master gives one man five bags of gold, and the man returns to share that he has gained five more. The next man is given two bags of gold and comes back with an additional two bags. The last man says he was afraid, so he just buried the gold and returns only what he was originally given.

We are all given varying levels of certain things in life: talents, time, money, skills, and other resources. God has gifted each of us in unique ways, but it is up to us to decide how will we use those gifts. Will we take a chance and pour ourselves into what He has called us to do, to be, and to stand for? Or will we let fear get the best of us and bury what we've been given?

God is like the master, waiting to see if we will be faithful to use what we've been given before He gives us more. Sometimes we can get so impatient, waiting for something bigger and seemingly more meaningful, that we lose sight of how effective we can be right where we are with what we've been given.

So maybe right now you feel like your life is small and isn't making much of a difference. It kind of reminds of me the story about the little girl who walked the edge of a beach that was covered in starfish that had washed ashore. She kept picking up starfish and throwing them back into the ocean, and a man said, "Why do you keep doing that? It's never going to make a difference."

She picked up another starfish, threw it back in the ocean, and replied, "It made a difference to that one."

Don't underestimate the impact your small acts of faithfulness and obedience can have in your life and in the lives of those around you. God very purposely created you for this time and in this generation, so let's do our best to be faithful with our gold.

THE ULTIMATE LIFE COACH

In their hearts humans plan their course,
but the LORD establishes their steps.

PROVERBS 16:9

It seems like I keep hearing a lot about life coaches. I think the first time I saw it was as some girl's job title when she was a contestant on *The Bachelor*, and I wondered at the time if that was a real thing.

And if that's a real thing, do I want you *to coach me how to live my life if you're a contestant on* The Bachelor? *Probably not.*

As it turns out, life coaches are real. People hire them to assist in setting goals, creating a life plan, and figuring out how to make the most of their lives. And none of that is necessarily a bad thing. Because the reality is, even if you don't have a formal life plan drawn up by a life coach, you probably have a plan in your head. I think we all do. We want to get a college degree, get married, start a family, find a good job, buy a house, and then decorate it according to whatever the latest trend on Pinterest may be—perhaps not in that order. We want to attain a certain level of comfort and stability for our family. We want our lives to make a difference, and so we make plans and set goals for ourselves.

And honestly, that can be good—because if you fail to make plans, then you may just find yourself lying on your couch for days on end watching Netflix. But I've lived long enough to know that we better hold our plans with open hands because there are so many times when God has totally messed up my plan. And that's a shame because I really thought I knew best, with my teeny tiny human brain that defaults to eating junk food and too much online shopping.

Yet it's our willingness to go to places or take steps we didn't anticipate that turn our lives into an adventure. And when we open ourselves up to the life God has for us to live, it's probably going to end up looking a lot different than what we originally planned or envisioned. It will be *so* much better because it will have a purpose and certainly be more than a life coach could have drawn up for us.

Day 34

STRONGHOLD

....

The LORD is my light and my salvation—
whom shall I fear? The LORD is the stronghold
of my life—of whom shall I be afraid?

PSALM 27:1

When I was a little girl, I was deathly afraid of the dark. I dreaded bedtime every night and can remember lying in my bed and letting my imagination run away with me as I conjured up all manner of monsters who might be in my closet or waiting for me under the bed. In the light of day, I always knew none of it was real, but every night I'd find myself in the same situation as I struggled to relax and fall asleep.

At some point, I came across Psalm 27:1, which reminded me that God is the stronghold of my life and that I have no reason to fear. It became a life scripture for me, a reminder that no matter what I face, God is with me and promises to be my light and my salvation.

Now that I'm a grownup, I don't worry about monsters under the bed. But I do have nights when all the "what ifs" dance in my head and keep me awake. *What if I get sick? What if something happens to Perry or Caroline? What if my parents get in a car wreck on their way back from Houston?* It becomes like an annoying song you can't get out of your head (I'm looking at you, "Total Eclipse of the Heart") as it repeats in my head as I jump from bad-case to worst-case scenario.

But that's when I pull out the verse that has comforted me since I was a little girl. "The LORD is my light and salvation—whom shall I fear?"

It doesn't mean that hard times won't come or that some of our fears couldn't happen, but it's a reminder that no matter what life may bring, we can rest in knowing that the Lord is our stronghold and in Him we can find rest and comfort.

A NEW HISTORY

....

"For I will pour water on the thirsty land, and streams on the
dry ground; I will pour out my Spirit on your offspring, and
my blessing on your descendants. They will spring up like
grass in a meadow, like poplar trees by flowing streams."

ISAIAH 44:3-4

I have a group of girlfriends that gets together for dinner every few months. We have been doing this for a long time We all know each other so well because we've lived a lot of life together. One of the common threads we share is that we all have some baggage in our families, whether it's our parents or our in-laws. We all wrestle with how to create a healthier future for our own kids. How do you keep the parts that are good and let go of the parts that have been so hurtful?

Whether intentional or not, we all have places in our past where we've been hurt or disappointed or betrayed. It's a difficult thing to reconcile when the people who should love us the most either can't or don't. Is that why the wounds that come from our families seem to hurt the deepest?

When I was pregnant with Caroline, I prayed that God would show me how to be a good mother, and He led me to Isaiah 44:3-4. I prayed for wisdom and discernment and the strength not to parent out of my deficiencies but to trust God to do a new thing in our family.

I've struggled with this so much over the years, but here's what I'm learning:

our history doesn't define our future unless we let it. We can break generational chains and ask God to create something new, a new legacy that will refresh our families like streams in what was once a dry, barren desert.

But the key to this is that we also have to forget the old things, to let go of the old hurts. Yes, those things were real and painful, but when we continue to hold on to our brokenness, it can consume our focus to the point that we lose sight of the new things God is trying to do through us. God specializes in fresh starts and promises to give us beauty where there was once ashes, so my prayer is that we trust Him and walk in what is new and refreshing to our family and our soul. Trust Him and walk to the future, knowing He holds it all in His hands.

ALL THAT IS WITHIN YOU

························

Bless the LORD, O my soul, and all that is
within me, bless his holy name!

PSALM 103:1 ESV

During my teenage years, we attended a church called Cathedral in the Pines. Isn't that a great name for a church? Especially because this was in East Texas and it was very literally a cathedral in the pines. This was back in the days when people went to church Sunday morning, Sunday night, and Wednesday night, and we were there every time the doors opened. Some of my motivation may have had more to do with whatever cute guy in youth group I happened to like that week, but whatever. God uses all things for His good, and my boy-crazy tendencies ensured I was in church three times a week.

Anyway, our pastor was a larger-than-life man named Pastor Dabney. And almost every Sunday, the choir would wrap up our worship time by singing, "Bless the LORD, O my soul, and all that is within me, bless His holy name!" Pastor Dabney would stand at the pulpit and belt it out in his large, booming voice. It is one of those memories that has stuck with me. I cannot read that verse or hear those words without hearing his voice in my head. It's a vocal memory reminiscent of James Earl Jones as Darth Vader saying, "Luke, I am your father." Powerful and strong.

The other day I heard a modern worship song that included those same words: "Bless the LORD, O my soul, and all that is within me, bless His holy name." I was struck by the phrase "all that is within me." The day I heard this wasn't one of my better days. I had all kinds of things going on in my head—fears, worries, insecurities. A veritable laundry list of all my failures.

But what hit me as I heard those words was that God wants *all that is within me*. He wants me to bring Him my darkest thoughts and my deepest dreams, the highs and the lows of my humanity, and to praise Him with it. When we come to Him, it's about everything in us praising His holy name, and that makes me more aware than ever of what I'm allowing in my life and heart and mind.

Am I living in such a way that *everything within me* is praising His holy name? Honestly, it depends on the hour and the day. But it's where my heart longs to be, because we have a God who loves us even when all that is within us doesn't seem very good. And even on those days, we can still praise His holy name.

Day 37

GOD IN YOU

·····································

Who is wise and understanding among you? Let
them show it by their good life, by deeds done
in the humility that comes from wisdom.

JAMES 3:13

Is it just me or does the world feel perhaps a *little* unhinged right now? Everyone is so angry, and we've never had so many ways to argue with each other. My Facebook feed is like a Dumpster fire, and I can't even deal with Twitter. Only Instagram holds any appeal, and that's mainly because I follow super edgy accounts like Dogs Being Basic, which is basically a showcase of dogs at their cutest and schmoopiest selves. Have you ever seen a dog who continually fails at jumping up on a couch? If not, then you haven't been living your best life.

I decided long ago that social media isn't the place for me to air my grievances or opinions. It's hard to truly hear someone's heart in only 140 characters, and my personal love language of sarcasm doesn't translate well, even with the best use of emojis. And the truth is, I don't expect anyone to listen to my opinion or so-called wisdom on a topic unless they know me and see something in the way I live that appears to have some value.

When I read James 3:13, I'm reminded to let people see Jesus in me through the way I choose to live my life. I'm challenged to remember to do good works in His name and for His glory and to walk in humility. My prayer is that I let

God speak the loudest in the way I love my family, the people around me, and the world at large. Because sometimes the wisest thing we can do is admit that we don't have all the answers—but that we know the One who does and the way we live looks different because of Him.

FOUR HUNDRED YEARS OF SILENCE

Be patient, therefore, brothers, until the coming of the
Lord. See how the farmer waits for the precious fruit
of the earth, being patient about it, until it receives the
early and the late rains. You also, be patient. Establish
your hearts, for the coming of the Lord is at hand.

JAMES 5:7–8 ESV

If we were to go around the room right now (let's pretend we're all in a room), I guarantee that each of us could tell a story about something we are either currently waiting on or hoping will happen in our lives. And there's a good chance it's something we almost find hard to speak out loud, because all of us have something we've lost hope in—our finances, relationships, children, marriage, work situations, or the world in general.

Sometimes it seems like it's the areas where we feel most hopeless that God seems silent. We wonder, *Where is He in the middle of our hopelessness? Where is our light in the darkness?*

From the closing words of Malachi in the Old Testament to the opening chapter of Matthew in the Bible, four hundred years of silence passed. SILENCE. Where was God? What happened during those four hundred years?

At the close of Malachi, Israel is back in Palestine after Babylonian captivity but under domination of Persia and Medeo. And by the time Matthew begins, Israel is under Roman rule. During those four hundred years, pagan empires rose and fell. Alexander the Great managed to conquer what seemed to be the entire world yet couldn't conquer Jerusalem. And the Old Testament was translated to Greek, which was pivotal to the Bible being translated for everyone to read and understand.

At the end of the four hundred years, people had grown tired of pagan faiths and were weary of the world in general. There was an air of expectancy as people began to wait and hope for the promised Messiah. All of these things worked together to create a world that was hungry and desperate for a change, a world that sensed its darkness and hopelessness. And when the time was just right, God sent His Son to earth as a baby boy.

When all hope was lost and the world was at its darkest—God showed up in a totally unexpected way.

This is a reminder to me that God's purposes never end and He is *always* working them out for our good. The world was hopeless . . . and that's when God showed up. That's what He did then and that's what He does now. He never changes. His love is steadfast, and His purposes and plans endure forever. When we find ourselves in the waiting seasons, it's good to remember that God is never silent. In fact, He's hard at work weaving together plans and purposes that will exceed our greatest expectations.

Day 39

THE ARMOR YOU HAVE

Then Saul dressed David in his own tunic. He put a
coat of armor on him and a bronze helmet on his head.
David fastened on his sword over the tunic and tried
walking around, because he was not used to them. "I
cannot go in these," he said to Saul, "because I am not
used to them." So he took them off. Then he took his
staff in his hand, chose five smooth stones from the
stream, put them in the pouch of his shepherd's bag and,
with his sling in his hand, approached the Philistine.

1 SAMUEL 17:38–40

We've all read about David killing Goliath at least a thousand times. It's a Sunday school classic, probably because it's everything we love in a story. A small shepherd boy who was just delivering lunch, an ugly giant who was tormenting an army, a little bit of trash talk, and then triumph over evil. If Bravo TV existed back then, David totally would have gotten his own reality show.

But here's what I love about the story that I completely missed when I was younger. Saul tries to equip David for battle by giving David his armor. And it isn't any old armor. Saul was the king, so you know his armor was made of the finest materials. Yet David quickly realized that it wasn't going to work for him. It was too big and bulky. David needed materials he had used before successfully as he killed the lions and bears that tried to attack his sheep.

So David grabbed his staff and five smooth stones as he approached Goliath. And, well, we know the rest of the story. Spoiler alert: things didn't go well for Goliath, but the birds of the air ate well that day.

I'm reminded that sometimes when I face big challenges, I'm waiting for God to equip me with big, fancy ways to fight them. Surely big problems call for elaborate solutions, right? Except they totally don't. Sometimes solutions are as simple as remembering that we come in the name of the Lord Almighty, the God of the armies of Israel, and so it's never about our power or our ability to fight a giant or having the fanciest armor. All we need is to remember that God is using all the little pieces of our life to prepare us for whatever we may face and that we never go into battle alone. Sometimes all it takes is five small stones and a big faith.

THE SPIRIT-
TRANSFORMED LIFE

··

"I will pour out my Spirit on all people. Your sons and
daughters will prophesy, your old men will dream dreams,
your young men will see visions. Even on my servants, both
men and women, I will pour out my Spirit in those days."

JOEL 2:28–29

The prophet Joel wrote these words almost a thousand years before Jesus was born and prophesied that a day would come when God would pour out His spirit on all people. This is pretty amazing in and of itself, but is especially incredible when you realize that Joel specifically included both women and servants in the prophecy at a time when women and servants were often overlooked. But since the Holy Spirit is essentially the very heart of God, it makes sense that He meant for every single one of us to experience the indwelling of His Spirit.

This is how God changes us. He pours out His Spirit on us, and we are never the same. His spirit in us transforms us.

In Acts 7, we read about Stephen being stoned to death for preaching about Jesus while a man named Saul gave his approval and persecuted the church. But in Acts 9, we read about that same man, Saul, experiencing Jesus for himself on the road to Damascus.

Saul comes face-to-face with the error of his ways and turns to Jesus right there on the road to Damascus. But it was when a man named Ananias arrived and said, "Brother Saul, the Lord Jesus—who appeared to you on the road as you were coming here—has sent me so that you may be filled with the Holy Spirit" (Acts 9:17) that Saul was truly transformed. God changed both his heart and his name, and the Apostle Paul became one of the most pivotal people in the history of the church and wrote a good part of the New Testament.

The Holy Spirit in Paul transformed him from a man who relentlessly persecuted Jesus' followers to a man who endured beatings and prison and all manner of hardships to ensure that the gospel of Christ was shared far and wide. When others heard that he had been converted, they struggled to believe it. Saul was notorious. They doubted whether he was really a believer and if his motives were pure.

Haven't we all feared that? That people will say, "Well, I knew her back when . . ." or "I remember when she was *the worst*" or "I don't believe she's any different than she used to be."

When we allow the Holy Spirit to truly transform us, the world may not understand. And Satan wants nothing more than to let our fear of who we *were* keep us from becoming who God *wants us to be*. The Holy Spirit takes all the unique ways God created us and uses them for God's will and purposes. It's through God's power that we become all that we were intended to be and all of our gifts are used.

God chose Paul to spread the Gospel of Jesus Christ because He knew Paul was stubborn and overzealous and knew the law better than just about anyone. God took every strength Saul had been using to persecute the church, transformed him by the Holy Spirit, and then used those same strengths to build His church.

And there are ways God specifically created each of us, experiences we've had, that He will use if we allow His Spirit to transform us, empower us, and equip us to make a difference in our lives and the lives around us. My prayer is that we allow the Spirit that has been poured out in us to help us run a race that is more fulfilling, more life-changing, and more inspiring than anything we could do on our own.

Day 41

RUNNING HOME

"While he was still a long way off, his father saw him
and was filled with compassion for him; he ran to his
son, threw his arms around him and kissed him. . . .

'Quick! Bring the best robe and put it on him. Put a ring on
his finger and sandals on his feet. Bring the fattened calf
and kill it. Let's have a feast and celebrate. For this son of
mine was dead and is alive again; he was lost and is found.'"

LUKE 15:20, 22–24

I grew up in church, so I can't remember the first time I heard the story of the prodigal son. It was just another Bible story like Noah and the ark, Joseph and the coat of many colors, or Moses and the parting of the Red Sea. I never gave it much thought.

As a teenager, I slowly turned away from the Christian foundation I had been given as a child. I had always stayed on the fringe of being really popular because I didn't drink or go to all the parties, and by my junior year I was sick of sitting on the sidelines of what I perceived to be all the fun things happening all around me. I jumped in with both feet and quickly found myself dating one of the most popular boys in school, going to all the good parties (you know, the ones that involved parents being out of town and kegs of beer), and rebelling against all I knew to be right.

My downward spiral continued throughout high school and well into college. I knew what was right, but I was so stubborn, and I felt like a voice was whispering to me that I was too damaged to go back now. I'd made too many mistakes, sacrificed too much, and I felt like there wasn't anything better for me.

As I became more and more unhappy with the choices I was making, I began looking for answers, something to make me feel not so empty and lost. One night during my senior year in college, I picked up a book called *No Wonder They Call Him the Savior* by Max Lucado. His account of the prodigal son rocked me to my core. I had never before understood how much God loved me, how much He wanted me, and how His grace completely covered every mistake I had ever made. A line in the book said, "No matter what you've done, no matter what you've become, please come home."

And I felt like God was speaking directly to me.

The next week, I attended a Bible study called Breakaway led by a student named Gregg Matte (who is now the head pastor of First Baptist Church in Houston). I walked into the room feeling a little intimidated, a little unsure of my footing in a church environment. But then a guy named Chris Tomlin (maybe you've heard of him) started leading worship and sang a song called "Grace Flows Down." I cried like a baby—not just a few tears but a full-on ugly cry. I didn't care how I looked, I didn't care who was watching, and I didn't care what it cost me because for the first time I realized that it had cost Him everything and He did it *for me*. And like the prodigal son, I went running home.

And the best part? My Father came running to meet me.

Day 42

DIFFERENT GRASS

··

I have learned the secret of being content in any
and every situation, whether well fed or hungry,
whether living in plenty or in want. I can do all
this through him who gives me strength.

PHILIPPIANS 4:12–13

Once upon a time, when I was a semi-high-powered career woman, I saved most my vacation time for December. I loved to have almost the entire month off during the holiday season. I could shop and bake and decorate to my heart's desire without having to worry about work pressure. I used parchment paper and baked homemade bread and pretended I was Martha Stewart, but with a better wardrobe and less skill.

It was always the best month. And every year, I'd think to myself that if only I didn't have to go back to work in January, life would be perfect. I wouldn't have anything to worry about. Life would be an idyllic fairy tale filled with rainbows, unicorns, and birds that sit on your finger and sing. Except maybe not the birds because their little bird feet kind of creep me out.

Fast forward to a few years later, and I found myself out of the professional workforce for the first time since college. People asked all the time if I enjoyed being a stay-at-home mom, and my answer was always yes.

I loved not having to balance so many responsibilities. I loved not feeling a cloud of pressure hovering over me at all times. I loved not having to worry about some doctor telling me he wouldn't prescribe my drug (I was a pharmaceutical rep), even if it was humankind's last chance for survival. And I loved not having to do expense reports on the worst expense report software in the history of ever. (I still have nightmares about forgetting to turn in my expense reports.)

I loved being able to lie in bed with Caroline in the mornings and watch cartoons. I loved making plans at the last minute to go to the park.

But there were no rainbows, unicorns, or creepy singing birds.

Because while, yes, I was so happy and blessed by this new phase in life, it wasn't the end of all my problems. It just created new sets of worries and concerns. I'd merely exchanged one set of issues for another.

I worried about our private insurance and monthly payments. I worried about the cost of gas and car insurance. I worried about spending too much at the grocery store or going out to eat too often. I worried about whether I was playing with Caroline enough and coming up with engaging activities. I worried that she wasn't learning her letters when I heard SuperWhy asking on TV for a fruit that started with an "A" and Caroline began yelling, "LEMONS!! LEMONS!!" I worried about keeping the house clean and the laundry done. (Of course, probably not as much as I should have.)

It all goes back to the oldest deception in the book—believing that the grass is always greener on the other side. In my mind, the stay-at-home mom side of the yard was lush and green and nicely fertilized with no mosquitoes and you never had to mow. Who could have a care in the world on that side of the lawn?

Women (or rather, humans) tend to do that. We look around us and compare our lives to others. Instagram is especially helpful in this regard. People's lives can seem so perfect and pretty from the outside, but do we have any idea what's really happening on the inside? All around us, people are hurting and lonely, but you'd never know just by looking at them.

The transition to being a stay-at-home mom made me realize that, short of God, nothing is perfect. Every situation has its burdens, it struggles, its worries.

I remember when Lance Armstrong won his 86th Tour de France or whatever. I watched him accept his trophy surrounded by his beautiful wife and kids and thought, *Wow. They HAVE IT ALL.* Shortly after that, I read that they had filed for divorce. Apparently what was happening on the inside was different from what was happening on the outside. It was a huge reminder to me that no one has it all together.

Life is made up of moments, and while some are perfect, some are not.

What I'm continually learning is to appreciate the blessings God has placed in my life, to live in this moment, even if it's not my favorite moment. I don't want to spend my life wishing for what someone else has. Because God, in His infinite wisdom, has something different *for me*. And I want to be content in trusting that He will give me what I need, when I need it.

Day 43

THE MIRACLE OF FORGIVENESS

....

Some men came carrying a paralyzed man on a mat and tried
to take him into the house to lay him before Jesus. When they
could not find a way to do this because of the crowd, they
went up on the roof and lowered him on his mat through the
tiles into the middle of the crowd, right in front of Jesus. When
Jesus saw their faith, he said, "Friend, your sins are forgiven."

LUKE 5:18–20

A dear family friend was dying of cancer, and her daughters called to ask where the Bible story was about the man whose friends lowered him through the roof to see Jesus.

After I mined my vast biblical knowledge (and Google) to give them the scripture reference, I read the story again myself. And what hit me was the realization that I'd always seen the miracle of the story as the paralyzed man being able to walk. That's not what it's about at all! The miracle is the forgiveness of the man's sins. The physical healing just demonstrated Jesus' power in a tangible way.

It was like something clicked. I realized that I spend so much time praying for *things*, for tangible demonstrations. I pray that God will do this or that, but I forget that the most incredible thing He can do has already been done—He paid the debt for our sins.

We are a new creation. Our chains have been loosed, and we are set free. That's something that no amount of chemo or surgery or new and improved medical treatment can give. It's only through Christ that we can truly be healed, truly be free, truly be changed and transformed, and truly conquer the grave.

Yes, we pray for the physical healing because miracles happen every day and because we don't want to say goodbye to our loved ones. But this story is a reminder to also pray for His will, His forgiveness, for Him to strengthen our faith and to help us find peace in knowing that He is all-powerful and sees things we can't see. He sees the eternal picture.

Even in the darkest night, we can find joy in knowing that the greatest miracle of all has already happened—we have been set free.

OUR TRUE HOME

....

"The thief comes only to steal and kill and destroy; I have
come that they may have life, and have it to the full."

JOHN 10:10

Several years ago, during December, we took a family trip to New York City. Getting to show Caroline the city at Christmastime will go down as one of my favorite memories ever, especially our visit to Santa Claus at Macy's on 34th Street. Watching her face light up as she told him what she wanted and Santa taking the extra time to discuss the Percy Jackson books she loved made it one of those magical moments I'll cherish always. It was one of those rare times when real life surprises you with so much joy.

And I guess that's part of why I couldn't stop the tears when we made it back to our hotel later that afternoon and turned on the news and discovered what had occurred earlier that day at Sandy Hook Elementary. Because while I was watching Caroline and my niece, Sarah, experience the very best of childhood magic and wonder, a school of precious littles, just sixty miles away, was experiencing horror beyond comprehension.

Honestly, even all these years later, it's too much. Too much sadness, too much agony, too much hurt to comprehend.

I hear bad and scary stories about kids and tend to mentally list all the reasons they could never happen to Caroline. I pay attention. I don't leave her home alone. I don't let her walk down the block without watching to make sure she arrives safely at her destination. I make sure I know everyone she encounters during a day.

But what happened that day at Sandy Hook shattered any illusion I had of being in control. Those parents dropped their babies off for a day at school. A day that should have been filled with learning to identify verbs in a sentence or adding numbers or eating paste like every other elementary school kid. And the unfathomable happened.

I don't have any answers because I don't think we'll understand this stuff here on earth. But here's what I do know: I know that this is not our home.

I know that the God in heaven is good and faithful and true even when nothing makes sense. And I know that we live in a fallen world filled with sorrow and tragedy and madmen capable of terrible things.

I know that there is no better time than Christmas to remember that God sent His Son into the world to save us all from darkness and sin and certain death. And I know that two tthousand years ago, the a baby's cry was the holy roar letting evil forever know that weeping may last for a night but joy will come in the morning.

One of the parts of the Christmas story often swept under the rug is the mass murder of innocent children at the hands of a crazed King Herod that caused Joseph and Mary to flee with Jesus to Egypt. There's no way to make that look pretty. No way to dress that up as part of the manger scene with wise men and shepherds and maybe a cow for good measure.

Yet it's there, in all its ugliness and darkness. It's easier to deal with because of time and distance. It's part of long-ago history. Pictures of those precious faces aren't strewn all over Facebook, but those babies in Jesus' time whose lives were cut tragically short left behind parents filled with unimaginable grief.

The truth is that our world is filled with darkness and always has been. Satan comes to steal and kill and destroy. And what feels more destructive and violent than the loss of innocent lives—lives that embody the very tenderness of

God, filled with so much light and promise and possibility and freckles scattered across their sweet faces?

I know that we are called to be a light in a dark world. And as much as events like Sandy Hook make me want to wrap my entire family in bubble wrap and spend the rest of our days within the walls of our home, we are *called* to spread the love of Christ and to share that hope and redemption and peace and purpose beyond what we can imagine available right now. Jesus came to earth in the form of a helpless baby, but He won't come back that way.

He'll come as a conqueror. And evil will be vanquished forever.

REFINING FIRE

But he knows the way that I take; when he
has tested me, I will come forth as gold.

JOB 23:10

I didn't grow up in an especially outdoorsy family—unless you count playing golf and sitting on the patio on a nice evening *outdoorsy*. So when I married Perry, I began to learn all manner of things about the outdoors that I had never known. Essentially, it was like City Barbie married Marlin Perkins.

Perry's family owned ranches during his childhood, so he spent a lot of time learning about land and wildlife. And one of the things he explained to me early on is that farmers and ranchers purposely burn a lot of their land every few years because it helps put much-needed nutrients back in the soil, which make the grass or crops or whatever come back stronger and healthier. This is called a "prescribed burn," and you are welcome for the free agricultural lesson you can use to impress your friends, who probably have lived their whole lives without needing to know that information.

Several years ago, Texas was in the middle of the worst drought in its history, and a huge wildfire spread through Bastrop, Texas. I drive through Bastrop any time I make the trip from San Antonio to College Station, and I've always loved the way the highway is cocooned on both sides by enormous pine trees as far as you can see. It's like a cathedral. The wildfires destroyed a large portion of those trees. When I made that drive a few weeks later, I was so sad to see nothing but charred remains. Yet only a year later, I made that same trip and saw firsthand what Perry had always told me. Yes, evidence of a fire remained, but there was also green, lush new growth all along the roadside.

It made me think about the way God works in our lives. Sometimes we let all this stuff in without even realizing it—life and stress and possessions and distractions. Our faith isn't as healthy as it used to be because all those things have sucked some of the life out of us. And sometimes it takes a little fire to get us healthy again, a little burning down of the distractions and disturbances and bad habits we've let creep in. Healthy new growth often sprouts up the best and strongest after our hearts have been through a fire. And sometimes, the most beautiful things come *after* the fire.

And just like gold is refined and molded by fire, God uses the fires in our lives to shape us and bring out everything we need to shine as we learn to trust Him more and see the beauty that only He can bring.

Day 46

CALLED FOR HIS PLANS

Jesse had seven of his sons pass before Samuel,
but Samuel said to him, "The Lord has not chosen
these." So he asked Jesse, "Are these all the sons you
have?" "There is still the youngest," Jesse answered.
"He is tending the sheep." Samuel said, "Send for
him; we will not sit down until he arrives."

1 SAMUEL 16:10–11

After it became clear that Saul was no longer fit to be king of Israel, God sent the prophet Samuel in search of his successor. And that's how Samuel found himself at the house of Jesse, taking a good, hard look at all of Jesse's sons. God had told Samuel that one of them would be His chosen king. Yet as Samuel looked at all seven of Jesse's sons standing in front of him, he knew something was missing. In fact, God told him, "The Lord does not look at the things people look at. People look at the outward appearance, but the Lord looks at the heart" (1 Samuel 16:7).

And so Samuel asked Jesse if these were all his sons. Jesse replied that his youngest son, David, wasn't there because he was tending sheep. They called for David, and when Samuel saw him, he knew that David was God's chosen king, so he anointed him right then and there.

What strikes me as I read this story is the realization David was either forgotten or overlooked—or both. Jesse was so sure that Samuel wouldn't be interested in David that he didn't even call him in from the fields. But God saw David's heart and knew he was up for the task even when David's own family didn't.

Haven't we all felt that way at times? Overlooked? Forgotten? Cast aside? Like we've been left out in the fields because no one thought we were worthy of being called in?

The anointing of David is a reminder to me to not let others determine what God wants to do through me. Don't let other people, even family members, make you feel like you aren't worthy of being called.

God is absolutely calling you to something, and you can rest assured that if He were done with you, you wouldn't still be here. And I'm assuming you're still here because you're reading this sentence.

Day 47

PARENTS ARE
THE WORST

··

When David returned home to bless his household, Michal
daughter of Saul came out to meet him and said, "How the
king of Israel has distinguished himself today, going around
half-naked in full view of the slave girls of his servants as any
vulgar fellow would!" David said to Michal, "It was before the
LORD, who chose me rather than your father or anyone from
his house when he appointed me ruler over the LORD's people
Israel—I will celebrate before the LORD. I will become even more
undignified than this, and I will be humiliated in my own eyes."

2 SAMUEL 6:20-22

The other night, I pulled into a parking spot to drop Caroline off at soccer practice. I was so worried about whether I had pulled in far enough that I ended up driving off the curb and back onto the street. Of course, several of Caroline's teammates witnessed this exhibition of stellar driving skills, and she gave me a time-honored, "MOOOOOM!!!" It was one of those moments as a teenager when you feel like you're the only human forced deal with parents who are clearly looking for new ways to humiliate you as they drive you all over town to your various practices and social engagements before returning home to cook you a well-balanced, nutritious dinner.

Parents are THE WORST.

The thing is, we never totally outgrow that part of us that dreads any sort of embarrassment. We all like to be cool, calm, and collected at all times. How else do you explain how mortified you feel when you trip on the sidewalk and feel the need to look around to see if anyone else saw and/or look at the spot where you tripped to make sure everyone sees that it *clearly* wasn't your fault but rather faulty sidewalk construction?

I think that's why I've always loved this moment in King David's life. He had just returned the Ark of the Covenant to where it belonged and is rejoicing—to the point that he forgets for a moment that he's the king and just dances down the street with pure joy before God. His wife, who happens to be King Saul's daughter (pro tip: don't marry the daughter of the king you replaced. In-law dynamics can be tricky enough), is disgusted by his behavior and mocks him. His reply is *the best*: "I will celebrate before the Lord. I will become even more undignified than this." In other words, "I don't care what people think of me because I will never stop worshipping my God."

I so want that to be my heart! I don't want to worry about what people think about how I choose to live my life, raise my child, and worship my God. I want to live a life fully abandoned to worshipping Him, honoring Him, and, yes, even occasionally dancing with joy to celebrate all He has done in my life. Don't you? Let's put on our dancing shoes.

Day 48

BEARING FRUIT

···

"I am the vine; you are the branches. If you remain in me and I in you, you will bear much fruit; apart from me you can do nothing."

JOHN 15:5

Caroline begged Perry to plant an orange tree in our front yard a few years ago. So he did. We live just far enough south that it has actually survived and even produces a ton of oranges each year. This would be great except for the fact that Caroline told us later that she really doesn't care for oranges. She just thought an orange tree would be cool. So I give most of our oranges to various friends and neighbors and to anyone who walks down our street and stops to ask, "Hey, is that an orange tree?"

The oranges are ready to be picked in December every year, but it's a process to get them to that point. In early spring, little blossoms begin to show up all over the tree that smell like the doorway to heaven. And then the blossoms eventually give way to the beginnings of fruit. The oranges start out as these tiny little green balls that continue to grow bigger and bigger until they resemble limes. Then their color begins to change from a deep green to a light yellow and then, finally, orange.

But here's what I think about as I watch that tree go through all the cycles of producing fruit—the tree isn't stressed about the process. Its roots go deep, the branches are connected to the trunk, and that's all the tree needs to blossom and grow and to fulfill its intended purpose.

It's so easy to get stressed about our lives and whether we're producing fruit. Are we raising good kids? Are we patient enough? Do we need to be drinking more fair trade coffee or helping to sell jewelry made by impoverished artisans? The thing is, we're like the orange tree in my front yard. When we are connected to the Source of all we need to sustain us—the roots of our faith—we can't help but bear fruit. There is no stress, but just remaining in Christ, who will equip us to be and do all He has intended.

And sometimes, just like our little orange tree, as the fruit is growing, it's hard to see the fullness of what it will become until, suddenly, it becomes clear that this is what we were intended to be from the very beginning. It just took small steps of faithfulness and abiding in our Source to get there.

FAITHFUL CARB-LOADING

Let us not become weary in doing good, for at the proper time we will reap a harvest if we do not give up.

GALATIANS 6:9

A friend of mine from high school is running the Boston Marathon and has been documenting her experience on Facebook. Yesterday was carb-loading day. I can totally get on board with that. Carb-loading day is what I like to call "Wednesday." The part of a marathon that truly troubles me is the running continuously for four hours part. *Four hours.* And that's considered a pretty decent finish time. Some poor saps out there will be running for closer to six hours—or if they're like me, *two days*—as they try to finish 26.2 miles.

The thing is, I absolutely believe in the importance of being physically fit. I've read all the magazine articles. I know it can lead to a longer life, better quality of life, and the ability to wear a swimsuit without wondering why a bunch of dum-dums let swim bloomers go out of fashion after the 1920s. But when it comes to exercise, I'm kind of like this guy John at church. Someone brought in a couple dozen doughnuts and set them on the same table as the coffee to share with everyone. John remarked to me later, "I went to go refill my coffee and accidentally ate two doughnuts before I remembered I'm supposed to be gluten-free." In that moment, I wanted to embrace him in a side-hug and whisper, "You, good sir, are my spirit animal." Because I would totally love to run a marathon someday and put one of those 26.2 bumper stickers on my car—except I keep forgetting that I don't like to run.

And that's the problem with exercise. If you want to see results, you have to keep doing it. You have to show up, do the work, sweat it out, and then rinse and repeat . . . FOREVER. While I'd like to say, "Ain't nobody got time for that," the reality is that I *do* have time. And because it's healthy, it needs to be *somewhere* in my list of priorities. The good thing is that if you don't give up, you eventually look in the mirror one day and realize you have arm muscles where you used to have none. Maybe you even dare to wear a pair of shorts for the first time in forever. I would say that perhaps you may even like the way you look in a swimsuit, but I don't believe that's actually possible. That's like the unicorn of dressing room experiences.

Exercise is a lot like life. Most of the time it can feel like doing the right thing is the most difficult thing. It can be hard to persevere through all the challenges life can throw our way and stay the course and follow the path that God has chosen for us.

But putting in the work, just like with farming (or so I've heard), leads to a harvest. Showing up and being faithful in all the small pieces of our lives has ramifications way beyond what we can even imagine while we're in the midst of taking care of the jobs, communities, churches, families, and people God has put in our path. Those are the non-glamorous things that produce a harvest that echoes throughout eternity. Which is also how long it will be before I like doing planks and push-ups.

Day 50

HOW TO LET GO

···

By faith Moses' parents hid him for three months after
he was born, because they saw he was no ordinary
child, and they were not afraid of the king's edict.

HEBREWS 11:23

You know what one of my biggest struggles is? Letting go of things. It's hard for me to surrender the things I love or want and to trust that God won't ask me to let go unless He has something bigger and better planned. Tim Keller says, "We can be sure our prayers are answered precisely in the way we would want them to be answered if we knew everything God knows." I totally agree with that, but it's still hard to trust when you can't see the whole story from beginning to end.

Jochebed was the mother of Moses. She gave birth to him at a time when Pharaoh had ordered that all Hebrew baby boys under the age of three be killed. But in Hebrews we read that Jochebed saw something in her baby Moses that led her to realize that he wasn't an ordinary child. Maybe she heard a whisper from God that He had great things in store for this baby boy. And so, by faith, Jochebed and her husband hid Moses for three months despite the orders from Pharaoh. Can you even imagine the stress of hiding a newborn for three months?

But the day finally came when she knew she couldn't hide him anymore. She had to do something even more difficult—she had to let her baby go and trust

God with the rest. Jochebed put her beloved baby in a basket and placed him in the Nile River. She watched to see what would happen, but the rest of the story was out of her hands. She had to believe that God would take care of one of the things she loved most.

As we learn in Exodus 2, God's plan was to have Pharaoh's daughter find Moses floating in his basket and raise him as her son. Even better, she unknowingly chose Moses' mother, Jochebed, to nurse him. So God not only protected the sacrifice Jochebed made but also gave her baby back to her in a way that ensured his safety. Moses ended up being raised in the most powerful household in all of Egypt, which paved the way for him to become the one God used to lead the Hebrews out of slavery and captivity. Jochebed's faithfulness set into a motion a plan that changed the pages of history. She couldn't have known that as she tearfully placed her baby in a basket, but she trusted anyway.

We've all had to let go of things: dreams, relationships, opportunities, people we love. We've had to accept answers to prayers that didn't turn out the way we wanted. Jochebed's story is such a reminder to me that God is always working out better things for us than anything we could imagine. And if we trust Him and let go, He will give back to us far more than what we have given up for Him.

Day 51

DOING A NEW THING

···

Now Israel loved Joseph more than any of his other sons,
because he had been born to him in his old age; and he
made an ornate robe for him. When his brothers saw
that their father loved him more than any of them, they
hated him and could not speak a kind word to him.

GENESIS 37:3–4

My grandmother used to say that all families are dysfunctional and in denial. I know what you're thinking. *What a warm sentiment. I'd love to have it cross-stitched on a throw pillow.* And I don't know that *all* families are dysfunctional and in denial, but I'm willing to bet that a not-small percentage *definitely* fall in that category, because family dynamics can be tricky and fraught with drama.

When we read the story of Joseph, we quickly learn that his family line was complicated. His father, Jacob, stole the birthright from his brother with the help of his mother and then had to run away. Jacob worked for his uncle, Laban, to marry Rachel, the woman he loved, only to be tricked into marrying her sister, Leah. Rachel struggled with infertility, but Leah gave birth to many sons. Finally, when Rachel gave birth to Joseph, he became Jacob's favorite son. Jacob made him a coat of many colors (maybe you've heard the Dolly Parton song). Joseph's brothers were fiercely jealous of him, which was only made worse when Joseph was dumb enough to tell them he had a dream where they all bowed down to him. Ultimately, his brothers wanted to kill him and instead threw him in a pit and sold him into slavery.

And you think *your* family is bad.

But it makes me wonder what happens to our hearts when the people who are supposed to love us the most don't. Or can't? Those are the wounds that can cut the deepest parts of us.

My own family has had its share of dysfunction. My parents divorced when I was in elementary school, and the years that followed were often tumultuous and filled with hurt. Maybe no one escapes their childhood without a few scars. But I determined that I wanted the family I built with my husband to be different and asked God to show me how to make sure my history didn't become my future.

Isaiah 43:18–19 says:

> "Forget the former things; do not dwell on the past. See, I am doing a new thing! Now it springs up; do you not perceive it? I am making a way in the wilderness and streams in the wasteland."

Joseph's story ends with the realization that God used every part of his story, even his brothers' hatred, for a larger purpose. God took what was broken and did a new thing.

And He can do the same for us if we trust Him enough to let go of those old hurts and find the beauty He offers in exchange.

IN HIS IMAGE

Then God said, "Let us make mankind in our image, in our
likeness, so that they may rule over the fish in the sea and the
birds in the sky, over the livestock and all the wild animals,
and over all the creatures that move along the ground."
So God created mankind in his own image, in the image of
God he created them; male and female he created them.

GENESIS 1:26–27

My daughter, Caroline, is in eighth grade right now. In fact, we are just about a month away from the end of the school year, which means she's about to be in high school, but I can't discuss that anymore because I feel like life is one of those old Folger's Coffee commercials and someone replaced my regular little girl who was just in kindergarten with this long, lanky teenager.

Anyway, none of that is the point I'm trying to make right now. The reason I brought up Caroline's academic career is because she's currently learning about the big bang theory in science. And last night as we sat at the dinner table, Caroline asked, "How can scientists believe that one big explosion made all of this? That doesn't even make sense. Why not just believe that God created it all?"

And I thought about the opening verses of Genesis, which describe in detail the way a loving God carefully created the heavens and the earth, and I wondered the same thing. Why do we fight so hard to come up with *any* explanation that is something other than God? Because when I look around at the uniqueness of creation—I mean hello-o-o, platypus—why wouldn't you believe that a divine being with an apparently hilarious sense of humor created it all?

Psalm 139 tells us that God knit each of us together in our mother's womb. He knows the number of hairs on our head and all the days ordained for us before they ever came to be. We are uniquely created and known by the God who put the stars in the sky and formed the seas and the winds. And to me, there is such comfort in knowing that's the God I serve. Because if He created us with that much care, then He certainly holds all the pieces of our lives in His hands.

Day 53

GLORY REVEALED

As he went along, he saw a man blind from birth. His
disciples asked him, "Rabbi, who sinned, this man or
his parents, that he was born blind?" "Neither this man
nor his parents sinned," said Jesus, "but this happened
so that the works of God might be displayed in him."

JOHN 9:1-3

I watched the movie *Jackie* the other day. It stars Natalie Portman as Jackie Kennedy and essentially follows the days shortly after President John F. Kennedy was assassinated. So many decisions had to be made about how and when to tell her children, the funeral service, and where the family would live since they had to vacate the White House almost immediately, all while Jackie walked through the heavy grief and trauma of losing her husband in such a violent, sudden way.

At one point in the movie, Jackie decides she needs to talk to a priest to help her process everything that is going on. The priest tells her the story of the disciples asking Jesus about the man who had been blind from birth and how they wondered if he was born blind due to his sin or the sin of his parents. Jesus responds that it was neither but that this happened so that the works of God would be displayed in the blind man's life. The priest explained to Jackie Kennedy that when we encounter hard times in life, we have an opportunity to let God's glory be revealed through us. The key is that we have to trust Him and lean on Him during those hard times, because life is going to come with its share of difficulties and only He can give us the peace we need to get through it.

Just this week, I found out that one of my dearest friends has been diagnosed with breast cancer. This comes on the heels of losing another best friend to breast cancer only eight months ago. And it can all feel like too much. *Why is this happening? When is it enough? Why her after all that our group of friends has already been through?*

It can be difficult to understand the purpose or the whys when life throws an unexpected curveball—a health issue, loss of a loved one, financial difficulties—but the story of the blind man helps me remember that God can use every situation in our life to allow us to show others His glory when we allow ourselves to trust in His plan.

THE YOU THAT ONLY YOU CAN BE

....

Joseph was well-built and handsome, and after a
while his master's wife took notice of Joseph and
said, "Come to bed with me!" But he refused.

GENESIS 39:6–7

Remember that time when you were placed in charge of a powerful man's household and then somebody wanted to sleep with you and you said no and found yourself in prison? Me neither.

But this was reality for Joseph. You'd think maybe being sold into slavery by your brothers would be the lowest point of your life, but I feel like being falsely accused after doing the right thing and then finding yourself in prison might be a close second.

Yet you know what you never hear Joseph say? "THAT'S NOT FAIR!" Joseph continued to trust God during all the tragedy and chaos in his life and always chose the high road—even though it appeared at times to be getting him nowhere except a prison cell.

I've heard it said that character is who you are when no one is looking. And I believe the key to living a successful life is to never compromise your integrity for any kind of gain.

Joseph could've slept with Potiphar's wife, and maybe no one would have ever known. But instead he risked it all to do the right thing. I just know it *feels* better to return the wallet filled with cash you found in a parking lot instead of keeping it for yourself and knowing it wasn't yours to keep. It's a reminder that living with integrity won't always be the easiest road, but it will always be the road that leads you where God wants to take you.

There is no job, relationship, or object worth losing who you are, because somewhere is a God-ordained opportunity waiting for the real you—the you that only you can be, the you that can sleep like a baby at night knowing you did the right thing even if no one noticed. No one applauded Joseph for his choice. In fact, he was punished for doing the right thing. But God saw, and ultimately, Joseph was blessed for being a man of character and integrity. God looks for those same traits in each of us, hoping to find us faithful in a million small ways that others may never even notice.

LISTEN FIRST

Everyone should be quick to listen, slow to speak and
slow to become angry, because human anger does
not produce the righteousness that God desires.

JAMES 1:19–20

When Caroline was little, she tended to overreact. And by overreact, I mean it was like something completely took over her body when she was angry. She'd flail and cry until she finally came to her senses a few minutes later and asked in her little toddler voice, "Happen? Happen?"

And we would tell her that what happened was she had temporarily lost her mind.

We began to teach Caroline about the appropriate response to situations and that it's overkill to have a level-10 response to a level-2 situation. Maybe when you hit your knee on the coffee table, you don't have to yell that we shouldn't even have a coffee table and that you want to break it to pieces. Instead, maybe express something more level-headed and reasonable such as, "Ow, that hurt!"

But here's the problem. I do the exact same thing—but on an adult level. It may not include as much crying and kicking on the outside, but it definitely has all the fury going on inside. Sometimes I get James's admonition to be quick to listen, slow to speak, and slow to become angry mixed up accidentally on purpose because I want to be right and am slow to listen and quick to speak. It's the curse of the sarcastic person. And it is certainly the hallmark of social media. Twitter is basically built on the premise of speaking quickly.

The problem is that my anger has never one time produced anything good. I've hurt someone's feelings, said words I later regretted, and ended up feeling like a horrible person. And I believe God knows that's what happens, which is why He is basically using James to remind us that we need to remember it's always best to listen first. This scripture helps me remember when I feel that anger start to rise up in me that I have never, not one time, regretted *not* saying the first thing that came to my mind and taking time to let a cooler head prevail.

Because no grown woman wants to hang her head in shame minutes after speaking, asking, "Happen? Happen?"

THE SPIRIT IN YOU

···

"I will ask the Father, and he will give you another advocate to help you and be with you forever—the Spirit of truth. The world cannot accept him, because it neither sees him nor knows him. But you know him, for he lives with you and will be in you."

JOHN 14:16–17

Jesus told His disciples that God would send His Holy Spirit to be with them. I'm sure they couldn't even comprehend what that meant at the time, but the Holy Spirit is how God equips us. He pours out His Spirit on us, and our lives are never the same. The Holy Spirit releases all the power of heaven into our hearts and our lives. All we have to do is ask.

The Holy Spirit is what truly transforms us into all that God has created us to be. We may not always understand and those around us may be thrown off by the decisions we make and the changes in our life once we accept Christ. And Satan wants nothing more than to let our fear of who we *were* keep us from becoming who God wants us *to be*.

I usually know it's the Holy Spirit when I do or say something much smarter or better or wiser than I actually am. A few months ago, I was at the grocery store and saw this young, frazzled mama pushing two toddlers in one of those horrendous racecar carts that are awesome in terms of kid likability but less than ideal in terms of actual maneuverability. Her kids were melting down, and I could tell she was at the end of herself when an older lady decided to chastise her for her lack of mothering skills. The older lady walked off, leaving this young mother in tears, and I felt the Spirit inside me telling me I needed to encourage her. It always feels a little awkward to approach a crying stranger in the frozen foods section of the grocery store, but I did it because I knew I was supposed to tell her that it was going to be okay, that she was going to make it through this. And when I ended up in the checkout line behind her, I felt God tell me I needed to give her a gift card to take care of her next grocery trip. I quickly purchased a gift card, handed it to her, and told her that God sees her and loves her. And I felt a million kinds of awkward because what if she thought I was some weird grocery store stalker?

But that's the thing about allowing the Spirit to be poured out in our lives: we have to be willing to die to our flesh. My husband always says that even with Jesus, we just aren't that good because our flesh is so weak. I feel like I prove that a thousand times a day. If there is anything good in me, it's because of the Holy Spirit.

And God specifically created each of us in ways that He will use if we allow His Spirit to empower and equip us.

On my own, so many times I have failed, but it makes all the difference when I remember that the Spirit lives within me and that Jesus promised we'll never be alone. He has given us a Helper, an internal Guide that lives within us, and we can count on that strength when our own has left us feeling weak and alone.

Day 57

HERD CHECK

....

Be sure you know the condition of your flocks,
give careful attention to your herds.

PROVERBS 27:23

Here's something I'm learning about having a teenager: keeping track of all the various ways they can screw up is a constantly moving target. At first I thought it would just be occasionally checking her text messages to make sure what she was sending and receiving was appropriate, but then we added in Instagram and Snapchat, and now I give thanks on a regular basis that social media wasn't a thing when I was growing up because I wouldn't have navigated it successfully at all. And by not successfully, I mean I probably never would've gotten a job due to the things I would've thought were hilarious to post when I was nineteen years old. It's weird what potential employers don't find amusing.

Then just when I think I've got it all figured out, I read some article on Facebook about how kids are making vapes out of USB ports or another mom mentions a show that all the kids are watching on Netflix that might be inappropriate and I realize I need to have another meaningful discussion with Caroline about what we allow and don't allow and what could potentially ruin her life and cause her to end up living in a van down by the river.

Because the thing about kids is that their frontal lobe isn't fully developed yet. It's a scientific fact that their judgment if often impaired and they can act impulsively without thinking about the consequences. If you have a teenager, you are yelling, "PREACH IT!" right about now. And so in some way, our kids are a lot like the sheep that shepherds tended back in ye olden days. They lack common sense and often don't realize that they might be putting themselves in danger.

Which is why I take this verse in Proverbs to heart. As parents, our families are our flock and we need to remember how important it is to keep tabs on what they are doing, where they are going, and the dangers that might be in their path and to daily ask God to give us the grace and wisdom to take care of our herd.

Day 58

RECOGNIZING THE HOLY SPIRIT

....

Simeon took [the baby Jesus] in his arms and praised
God, saying: "Sovereign LORD, as you have promised,
you may now dismiss your servant in peace. For my
eyes have seen your salvation, which you have prepared
in the sight of all nations: a light for revelation to the
Gentiles, and the glory of your people Israel."

LUKE 2:28–32

Chances are good that if you're reading through this devotional (and have made it to day 58), you are familiar with the Christmas story. Not *A Christmas Story*, where Ralphie gets his tongue stuck on the flagpole and Randy shows Mommy how piggies eat, although that's a good one, but the official Christmas story, where Jesus is born in a manger to a virgin named Mary.

We all know about the manger and the shepherds and the wise men, but I think a fascinating aspect of the story gets overlooked because it happens just a little further down the page in Luke 2. It's the story of Simeon and the prophetess Anna.

The scriptures tell us that Simeon was waiting for the consolation of Israel, that the Holy Spirit had revealed to him that he wouldn't die before he saw the Lord's Christ and that the Holy Spirit was resting on Simeon. In fact, the Holy

Spirit is what moved Simeon to go to the temple courts on the day Mary and Joseph brought Jesus there. And because Simeon had been looking for Jesus, he knew immediately that he was in the presence of God.

Then there was Anna the prophetess. We read that Anna never left the temple and worshipped day and night. So what do Anna and Simeon have in common? In a temple that was most likely brimming with people that day, they were *the only two* who realized they had just come face-to-face with God in the flesh. They recognized God even though He showed up in a way that was completely unexpected and probably different than they had imagined.

And I know that the reason why they were able to look at this tiny baby and see the face of God is because they were filled with the Spirit. This wasn't a way they lived just on the Sabbath or when life brought difficulties. It was the way they lived each day of their lives.

Simeon and Anna are a reminder to me that when we spend time with God, when we allow ourselves to be filled with His Holy Spirit, we are able to recognize when He is at work. We know Him when He shows up, even if it looks much different than we expected. Do I live that way? Do I recognize Him, even when He surprises me? My honest answer is probably no more often than yes. Sometimes I realize the ways God is working only after the fact, but Anna and Simeon are a challenge to me to live in such a way that I am always waiting and hoping for the moment God shows up.

Day 59

DO NOT BE AFRAID

··

But the angel said to her, "Do not be afraid, Mary; you have
found favor with God. You will conceive and give birth to a
son, and you are to call him Jesus. He will be great and will
be called the Son of the Most High. The Lord God will give
him the throne of his father David, and he will reign over
Jacob's descendants forever; his kingdom will never end."

LUKE 1:30-33

So that's an announcement that would blow your mind.

I think about Mary and how young and inexperienced she was when the angel dropped this bombshell in her lap. I think of times in my life when I've prayed for God to use me in this way or that way—and then I look at Mary. As far as we know, she didn't ask for this role in God's plans. I mean, who could come up with that?

Dear God, if You ever decide to send Your Son to earth as a baby to save all of humankind, please let me be His mother.

God simply showed up in her life, and she became part of His plan. This tells me that God saw something in Mary's heart and spirit and knew she would be faithful even when asked to do something that sounded crazy.

It makes me wonder, when God calls us to that crazy thing or hard place or leads us to something new and unexpected, do we trust Him? Do we have hearts that are open and willing to go where He leads—no matter the cost? Can we voice the words of a young Mary, who simply said, "I am the Lord's servant"? So many times in the Bible, we see God speak to much older and supposedly wiser people who push back with all the reasons they can't do what He's asking, and yet here is Mary, with a willing heart, who doesn't ask a single question or show fear, other than to wonder how she could become pregnant since she was a virgin.

It's also a great reminder to me that we don't have to be fearful or stress out over what God is calling us to do. He will show up and lead us where He wants us to go. We just have to have a heart that's willing to follow Him.

Day 60

AT THE
WATER'S EDGE

··

When the Israelites saw the mighty hand of the Lord
displayed against the Egyptians, the people feared the
Lord and put their trust in him and in Moses his servant.

EXODUS 14:31

I can't count how many times I have looked at what appears to be an insur-mountable obstacle and let fear and doubt overwhelm me. How many times have I heard myself say, "That's impossible!" or "There is NO WAY that situation can be fixed!"? The answer is TOO MANY.

The problem is that when tough times come, I tend to trust in what I can see and to forget what I believe. And we see in Exodus that the children of Israel were no different as they wondered aloud why God didn't just leave them in Egypt to die instead of bringing them out to the desert. Essentially, humans have been the very same from the dawn of time. We pray for God to help us figure out what to do about our job situation and then freak out when we get laid off and have to find a new opportunity. We ask for God to show up in our lives and feel like we're going to lose our minds when we have to take on a new challenge. We lose sight of the God we serve because we are blinded by the fears in front of us that become all we see.

My dear friend Jen fought a valiant battle against breast cancer that she ultimately lost in August 2016. She kept a blog of her experience, and in one of her posts, she compared her journey to that of the Israelites as they faced the vastness of the Red Sea.

> I couldn't imagine how the Israelites ran headlong toward the sea not knowing if it would open—but yet trusting the Lord to deliver them. I thought about how if the sea had parted two hundred yards before they arrived, it wouldn't require the same faith. I admire them. And I thought of how I feel like people give me too much credit for joy and peace and grace in this season but that it's truly HIM that has opened the seas and provided a smooth path in the face of death. And I've seen Him provide supernatural peace and grace.

As I read Jen's words, I was so challenged by her faith amid the realization of what she was about to face. Ultimately, she knew that the peace and joy she felt wasn't to her credit but was a testament to the faithfulness of a God who gives us what we need, exactly when we need it. He parts the seas just in time, He stills the storm just when it's about to overtake us, and He makes the path smooth even if it's a path we never imagined ourselves on.

He's just waiting for us to be obedient enough to take the first steps to the water's edge.

WHAT IF YOU SAID YES?

....

Jesus looked at him and loved him. "One thing you
lack," he said. "Go, sell everything you have and give
to the poor, and you will have treasure in heaven.
Then come, follow me." At this the man's face fell.
He went away sad, because he had great wealth.

MARK 10:21–22

I've always thought the story of the rich young ruler is so poignant. This wealthy young man runs to Jesus, falls to his knees, and is excited to learn more about His teachings. Jesus lists off the commandments, and the ruler proudly asserts that he has kept all of them. But Jesus looks past the surface and tells him that he must sell everything he has and give it to the poor. The young ruler decides almost instantly that this is a step too far and walks away sad.

My thoughts go to two places: I wish Jesus could've met him halfway. Maybe asked him to give up a little of his wealth. You know? Baby steps. But then I also wish the rich young ruler could've seen that what he would gain by following Jesus would ultimately be so much more than any comfort he'd find in his worldly possessions.

And I think those are my thoughts because I have been the rich young ruler.

I have run to Jesus time and time again, excited about the possibility of a new adventure or ministry and then ultimately decided it was more than I wanted to take on. I have patted myself on the back for how good I am. I mean, just last week I didn't even say my favorite cuss word when that lady cut me off in traffic and almost caused a wreck. I am like an angel on earth. I have built myself up, only to realize that anything good in me is really just a momentary illusion when I come face-to-face with the holiness of God.

Sometimes, as much as we love God, we are limited because we hold on to things He has asked us to surrender. God invites us into this new thing, but we grip our wealth, our fears, our insecurities, our safety nets so tightly because we don't really believe that God is going to give us everything we need. And the reality is that He is going to give us *so much more*.

How different might that rich young ruler's life have looked if he had said yes? How different would *our lives* look if we said yes? What if we took the leap, let go of the familiar and comfortable, and said yes to Jesus? He is just waiting to take us to places we never could have imagined.

Day 62

LOVE FOR SMALL BEGINNINGS

Do not despise these small beginnings, for
the LORD rejoices to see the work begin.

ZECHARIAH 4:10 NLT

Until about two years ago, Perry and I had attended the same church since Caroline was a baby. And it was a church we'd had ties to long before that. It was a great place for us for all those years. We were involved with different ministry groups, learned so much, made new friends, and there was a time when I couldn't imagine we'd ever go anywhere else.

But then something began to shift. At first I thought it was just my own issues, until one night when Perry and I talked and realized we were both feeling the same things. I can't even tell you what the exact feeling was other than just a little bit of restlessness regarding church that we hadn't experienced in a long time. So we began to pray about it and agreed to see what happened next. And what happened was that Caroline moved up to the junior high youth group and began to enjoy church more than she ever had during the days of elementary Sunday school. We agreed that was the most important thing and decided it meant we should stay put.

Then a few weeks later, the youth director sent out an email informing parents that the youth group would no longer meet on Sunday mornings and would instead meet on Wednesday nights. And here's the thing. That schedule wasn't going to work for us since the church is about a thirty-minute drive from our house on a Sunday morning and takes even longer when you factor in week-day traffic. Plus, Caroline admitted she never really got to know the other kids because none of them are from our neighborhood or attend her school and what she really wanted was to go to church closer to home.

Our familiar little nest was being shaken because God was calling us out of our comfort zone. It's those times in life when you either allow God to help you fly or fall flat on your face. And I have chosen the latter more times than I care to admit.

As we talked one night over dinner, what became clear was that we all had a desire to attend church in our neighborhood, with the people we go to school with and grocery shop with and see every day. We live in a small community in the middle of San Antonio, and we had no doubt that God was calling us to be a part of something right here and not thirty minutes away. Our hearts were increasingly drawn close to home. The problem was that we didn't know of a church that would be the right fit for us. Then one night, as we discussed it for the twenty-third time, Caroline declared, "Maybe we should start a church!"

What?

No. Just no.

I am not a church plant kind of person. I am not organized. I am not overly spiritual. I have never won a Bible drill contest. I have never even sung in the choir, unless you count my brief stint in mixed choir in seventh grade, which sounds much more impressive when I tell you that we sang "Human Nature" by Michael Jackson, complete with extensive hand motion choreography.

So I did the supportive mom thing by essentially patting her on the head and saying, "Aw, that's a sweet idea," while everything inside me was screaming, "PLEASE GOD DON'T MAKE US START A CHURCH! I DON'T WANT TO

START A CHURCH!" And I knew Perry was thinking the exact same thing by the way he looked at me across the table.

But it was one of those things—you know those things—that just burned a hole in my heart. And I knew—I KNEW—even though I tried to ignore it, that there was something to it. Out of the mouths of babes and junior high kids and all that.

At the same time this was going on at our house, some acquaintances who also happen to be immensely talented worship leaders, August and John, were feeling called to something new. August was at another church at the time, and Perry and I just happened to decide to attend that church on Easter Sunday, specifically because we knew the music would be great since August was leading worship. She saw us across the room that morning and came over to say hello and then mentioned that she was feeling so restless and like God was calling her to something new. I stared a hole into the side of Perry's head as August said those words, and I knew at that moment that God was about to do something. I was excited and scared and filled with wonder and nauseous all at the same time. I have never identified more with Moses in Exodus 4:13 when he said, "Oh, my LORD, please send someone else."

But Perry and I began to watch all these pieces fall into place. Pieces that we'd always cited as the reason we could never start a church. Where would we find a good worship leader? Where would we meet? What about the fact that neither of us wanted ministry to be our full-time job? Would anyone even want to come to a new church? What about how I like to sleep in on rainy Sunday mornings? All those things just seemed insurmountable.

And I realize now that that sounds ridiculous because, well, GOD. It turns out that when He says in Ephesians 3:20 that He will do more than you could ask or imagine, He means it. That's why it's more than you can imagine.

Because you can't imagine it.

We met with August and John about a week after Easter and discussed the logistics of what it would take to start a simple Sunday morning worship service.

And we all agreed that none of us were looking at this as a vocation but rather as creating an organic gathering of people who wanted to come together for worship and teaching with their families each Sunday morning right in our neighborhood. Kind of like the first churches in Acts, we wanted it to be about the people and not the place. I'd felt so strongly over the previous year God reminding me that the way to change your world is to start in your own community, to invest in the lives of the people around you, and that's what we wanted to do. We gathered in our living room to pray and agreed we would give it thirty days. The thirty-day church experiment. Sounds like a good blog post title.

As I write this, we are about to celebrate two years.

The past two years have caused me to question my sanity, my selfishness, my spirituality, and God. I will confess that on at least one Sunday morning, I have said aloud to God, "I HATE THIS. I wish You never would have called us to do this." And then ended up in tears an hour later when I looked at the group of people who believe in what we're doing and show up to help us make coffee and set up chairs and greet people as they come through the door. Starting this church or worship service or whatever we call it has been the greatest and hardest and best and worst thing I have ever done, sometimes within a five-minute span of time. It has stretched my faith in ways I never imagined and ultimately leaves me feeling so grateful that we have a God who uses us in spite of ourselves. Never underestimate what God can do with small beginnings. It's those very small steps of faith that often lead us to the bigger things in life.

THE GLORY IN OUR MIDST

·····································

And I lifted my eyes and saw, and behold, a man with a measuring
line in his hand! Then I said, "Where are you going?" And he
said to me, "To measure Jerusalem, to see what is its width and
what is its length." And behold, the angel who talked with me
came forward, and another angel came forward to meet him
and said to him, "Run, say to that young man, 'Jerusalem shall
be inhabited as villages without walls, because of the multitude
of people and livestock in it. And I will be to her a wall of fire all
around, declares the Lord, and I will be the glory in her midst.'"

ZECHARIAH 2:1–5 ESV

The world tells us we have to do it all, be it all, and achieve it all. We need to do big, important things to leave a legacy, all while looking fabulous and being a size four and raising kids who are fluent in at least two languages and are in all the gifted classes. Our houses must be straight out of Pinterest, our dinners need to be clean and healthy, and our Instagram accounts should to be full of beautifully filtered photos that catch every single moment of our kids' lives or they'll end up in therapy wondering why they don't have an Instagram book like all the other kids.

We are a generation of women that has never worked harder to have it all and yet goes to bed most nights worrying that we aren't enough. We are constantly asking "Why?" We are constantly measuring. It doesn't matter if you're single, married, rich, poor, old, young, in college, or out of college. Every human heart struggles with this. We are always looking around to see how we measure up against everyone around us and usually focusing on all the ways we fall short.

And I believe our struggle with wondering if we are enough goes back primarily to how much we trust God. We aren't struggling because of the specifics of our circumstances as much as because we fail to trust God to provide what we need and to show us where we're supposed to go and what we're supposed to do. That's why discontentment surfaces in our lives in all the ways it does. Deep down, we struggle so much with believing that God will lead us to what is best for us.

Our internal voice whispers that we'll never be enough, and so we work and worry and feel like we must do something big, something huge to prove our worth and to make sure our life matters. We think we have to host a conference, start a movement, adopt fifteen kids, or fight human trafficking to really matter. And these are all great, but they can cause us to lose sight of the small gestures that can also change a life—taking dinner to a sick neighbor, smiling at a waitress who's having a bad day, reading to your kids before bed, or simply praying for someone going through a rough time.

If you're like me, you can spend a lot of time looking around at what everyone else is doing or all the ways they appear better. We measure. We measure our insides by other people's outsides—and that's never a fair assessment. We don't know what others are going through, how they've been hurt, the struggles they face. We see people's best self on social media and assume they're all winning at life and leaving a lasting mark. We constantly see the "Everything's great!" version of other people's lives . . . while living the reality of our own lives, which may often feel mundane and purposeless.

A few weeks ago, I ran across these verses in Zechariah as I was reading my Bible. I can't even explain how I found myself in Zechariah because I sometimes can't remember if it's a real book of the Bible or one I made up in my head because it *sounds* like a name that should be a book of the Bible.

It hit me that we spend so much time doing *the same thing*: we are constantly measuring our "city." Is it big enough? Does it need more? How does it compare to other cities? Does my city have a kitchen that looks most likely to get pinned on Pinterest? Do people like my city?

What would happen if we began to live in a way that we stopped building walls around ourselves and let others see who we really are? What if we set aside the highlights reel and showed raw footage? To see where we are broken and where we are hurting and where we feel like we aren't enough? When we speak those things out loud, they often lose their power. But when we keep them hidden, they only grow because we are always our own worst critic.

What if we lived as if we truly believe God has given us a life without walls because He has plans for us that go beyond anything we can measure or imagine and promises to be the glory in our midst?

I believe God wants to make our city—our life—so big that walls can't contain it. He wants us to have peace and contentment that won't require us to put up walls of protection and spend our lives afraid of being vulnerable and real as we stop measuring the width and depth of our life. He will be our protection. He will be the wall of fire all around. He will be the glory in our midst and will whisper to us that our life, no matter how small it may seem to us, is enough because He is enough.

Day 64

WOMEN AT THE WELL

....

Jesus replied, "Anyone who drinks this water will soon
become thirsty again. But those who drink the water
I give will never be thirsty again. It becomes a fresh,
bubbling spring within them, giving them eternal life."

JOHN 4:13–14 NLT

Jesus had been traveling all morning. Around noon, He came to a well. It was hot and dusty, and He needed a drink. And that's when He encountered a woman at the well.

Here's what Jesus knew: she was at the well at the wrong time of the day. Women typically gathered water in the morning, not during the heat of the day, and so this woman had chosen to go at noon for a reason. Perhaps she had gone in the heat of the day because she thought no one else would be there.

Except that on that day, Jesus was there.

Jesus knew she would be coming to the well at that time—and He knew even more about her and the Living Water she truly needed. God always meets us where we are. He specializes in meeting us in our brokenness. We may think life has brought us to a certain point because we're just looking for water, but Jesus meets us there because He knows we are looking for healing, security, and love.

Ultimately, we are all the woman at the well. Jesus shows up in our lives, wherever our well may be, and offers us Living Water. He offers us everything we need, yet we often keep looking for all these other things to fill us up—our kids, our marriages, our finances, our homes, and our good deeds. I believe He looks at us with love and asks, "Aren't you ready for the real thing that will make you feel full?"

How deeply have we buried our hope, our faith, and our dreams that we don't think anyone can salvage them? What are the wells in our life? And do we trust Jesus to meet us there?

When I read in verse 15 the woman say to Jesus, "Give me this water," I remember how lost I felt in my late teens and early twenties. I was searching for anything other than God to fill me up. I was longing for some sense of family and belonging and security that I had no idea how to find. I looked for it in alcohol and guys and popularity and in trying to look a certain way. When I walked into Breakaway Bible study at Texas A&M University, I came face-to-face with Jesus and exposed all my brokenness. I couldn't stop crying. And I knew I'd finally found the Living Water I didn't even know I was looking for.

That's the grace of God. He meets us at the wells of our lives and gives us everything we need and so much more.

Day 65

HOLY WHITE COUCHES

Take your everyday, ordinary life—your sleeping, eating,
going-to-work, and walking-around life—and place it before
God as an offering....Don't become so well-adjusted to your
culture that you fit into it without even thinking. Instead, fix
your attention on God. You'll be changed from the inside out.

ROMANS 12:1–2 THE MESSAGE

About three years ago, I made a mistake of epic proportions and let a designer friend talk me into buying a white couch. And I really can't put the sole blame for this purchase on her because, the truth is, I'd been pinning living rooms with white couches on Pinterest for months, along with doing Google searches like "How hard is it to clean a white couch?" "Am I crazy for wanting a white couch?" and "White couch: friend or foe?"

Every blog post I read about having a white slipcovered couch raved about how it was so easy to maintain. Sure, it gets dirty, but you just take those slip-covers off, throw them in the washing machine with bleach, and your couch is good as new! *Good as new!* In fact, it's even better because you have the smug satisfaction of knowing that it's cleaner than your neighbor's couch. Who knows what horrors lie within that dark taupe fabric.

The day the white couch was delivered was perhaps second only to the day my daughter was born on the scale of best days ever. My living room looked like it was ripped straight from Pinterest, and we all know Pinterest was basically created to make women everywhere feel like we aren't living up to our potential. But for that one glorious day (let's be honest, it was more like two hours) I defied every teacher who wrote "Does not work to full potential" on my report cards— because I was, as Whitney Houston sang, EVERY WOMAN. It was all in me.

But then life happened. Perry came home from a long day of landscaping and innocently sat on the couch, leaving behind a bottom imprint made of dust and grime. "OH NO! THE COUCH!" I cried as I wiped my hand across the cushion furiously, trying to erase the dirty mark. Perry looked at me with pity as he remarked, "Well, this couch is going to work out beautifully. Totally worth the money. Who needs a couch you can actually sit on?"

I realized I'd made a strategic wife error, so I immediately switched into a more laid-back mode. "Well, the beauty of this is that it's all slipcovered! It's a wash-and-wear couch! It doesn't matter if it gets dirty because I'll just wash it with bleach! This is the best money we've ever spent! I promise!" But less than a week later I had some girlfriends over. One of them accidentally spilled an almost full drink on the center cushion, and I played the role of gracious hostess as I explained, "It's no big deal because BLEACH!"

The next morning, I stripped all the slipcovers off, washed them for the first time, threw them in the dryer, and then began putting them back on the cushions. That's when I discovered that all those white couch evangelists are either gluttons for punishment or in much better physical shape than me because people have finished triathlons with less sweat and exertion than it took me to get those slipcovers back on the cushions. There was profanity involved. I tore my clothes and covered myself in sackcloth and ashes.

But I couldn't admit to Perry that I'd made a costly tactical mistake. Even as he occasionally declared, "Babe, we aren't white couch people," I would insist that we were. We are clean. We shower. And look how good that couch looks for all of thirty-eight seconds once every three months when I muster the inner fortitude to wash, rinse, and repeat.

I finally made a tearful confession to Perry months later, "I can't do this. I cannot live like this. BABE, WE ARE NOT WHITE COUCH PEOPLE! *ERRBODY BE SO TIRED OF THIS WHITE COUCH!*"

He hugged me, and I'm sure all manner of "I told you so" comments were raging inside his head, but he is a smart man and just said, "Why don't we look into getting a new couch?" And with that, I ordered a brown leather couch so fast it would make your head spin. Brown. I am a brown-couch-that-can-be-wiped-clean kind of person. It's not nearly as Pinterest-worthy, but it has restored my delicate mental balance (although I'm still disappointed I wasn't up to the challenge). Maybe those teachers were right after all. I'm not living up to my potential.

But you know what I was doing with all my visions of what life should be, could be, and ought to be based on Pinterest? You know what we all do when we sit around thinking about our Fantasy Someday? We miss the holiness of this moment we're living right now. You miss that you have a husband who loves you enough to agree with your dumb white couch scenario and that you had some good laughs even when that couch was covered with muddy dog prints. There will never be another moment like it. And even if that makes you think, *Thank God, because my life currently stinks*, remember that there are still lessons to be learned, character to be built, and stories that will be shared about where you are *right now*.

God takes all of it—the mundane and the ugly, the clean couch and the spills, the ordinary and the occasional extraordinary. And when we allow Him to add His grace, mercy, and outrageous love, He makes a brushstroke there and adds some color here and paints it all into one glorious work of art that only He can achieve in that moment—in our homes, our neighborhoods, our classrooms, our communities, and our world. No one else can live our story, even when it's messy, even when it drives us crazy. And those are often the very moments you'll look back on and realize were what made it special.

Day 66

WORDS LIKE HONEYCOMB

....

Gracious words are a honeycomb, sweet to
the soul and healing to the bones.

PROVERBS 16:24

Two years ago, Perry and I, along with another couple, started a new worship service in our community. It has been one of the best and hardest things we've ever done. It can be difficult enough to get your family to church on Sunday morning and still like them by the time you walk through the church doors, but it adds a whole other layer when your family is actually the one in charge of setting up chairs and making the coffee and, oh yeah, preaching the sermon.

And so a few days ago, we found ourselves in the midst of some burnout. Disillusioned by another Sunday where it felt like not as many people showed up as we'd hoped for combined with just being tired from life in general, we had less than stellar outlooks on all things ministry related. But then August, our worship leader, called to tell us about a conversation she'd just had with a young woman who's been attending our service. This woman had shared with August how disappointed she and her husband had been as they visited church after church and couldn't find a place that felt right. But then they walked through our doors and knew after the first service that they'd found a place that was home. She'd raved about the sweet, simple spirit of God that filled the building and the way we all serve unselfishly (she's obviously not a mind-reader). Her kind words of encouragement were exactly what we needed at a time when we felt like throwing in the towel and calling it a day.

And it reminded me that just because someone doesn't look you in the eye and say, "Hey, you know what? I really need an encouraging, kind word right now," doesn't mean that their soul isn't craving a gracious word from another person. Sometimes the best thing we can do for another person is to take the time to tell them that they matter and that we see them and to fill them up with a little bit of kindness.

Day 67

FEARFULLY AND WONDERFULLY MADE

....

For you formed my inward parts; you knitted
me together in my mother's womb. I praise you,
for I am fearfully and wonderfully made.

PSALM 139:13-14 ESV

M y daughter, Caroline, is almost fourteen years old. Let's not dwell on that because she was three just yesterday and I'm not sure what has happened to the time. Whatever it is, it's basically the polar opposite of what Michael J. Fox did in *Back to the Future*.

The other night, she had an awards ceremony at school that required her to actually brush her hair and put on a dress. These are not activities she regularly engages in because she is a tomboy and prefers athletic wear and a ponytail at all times. When she walked out of her room all dressed up, I was stunned at how much of myself I see in her. I normally think of her as my husband's mini-me, but with her hair down and a little bit of lip gloss, it was easier to see the features she inherited from me. And I marveled at how God knits these babies together that end up being the perfect blend of all the individual qualities of their parents along with enough of their own temperament and personality to make them totally unique.

It made me think of Psalm 139, where David proclaims that he is "fearfully and wonderfully made." Most mornings I don't look in the mirror and think, *Wow. I am fearfully and wonderfully made*—usually because I'm too busy thinking, *So if I just got a little Botox right here, maybe I'd look less like the crypt keeper.*

When you look at the original Hebrew, *fearfully* means "with great reverence and heartfelt interest," and the word *wonderfully* means "unique and set apart." It makes me realize how much love, thought, and concern went into our unique design as God carefully created each of us. We are His masterpieces, walking around with flesh and blood.

And if we let that really sink in, we can comprehend maybe just a little bit how much He loves and cares for us. None of us is here by random chance. We were knit together with great reverence and deep emotion by our Creator—every fiber of our being. He could have made anything, but He chose to make *you*—with all your quirks and freckles and personality. For me, that realization shifts my perspective when hard times come or I feel insecure and bad about my "laugh lines" and I'm tempted to wonder if He cares. Of course He does! He's the one who knit us together from the beginning and continues to hold all the pieces of our lives in His hands.

Day 68

LOOKS LIKE A DESERT

··

The hand of the Lord was upon me, and he brought
me out in the Spirit of the Lord and set me down in the
middle of the valley; it was full of bones. And he led me
around among them, and behold, there were very many
on the surface of the valley, and behold, they were very
dry. And he said to me, "Son of man, can these bones
live?" And I answered, "O Lord God, you know."

EZEKIEL 37:1-3 ESV

A friend of ours tells this story from his childhood that always makes us laugh. His dad was a ranch realtor in South Texas back in the late 1950s. It was a time when South Texas was enduring a historic drought and the land was scorched and dry. Selling ranch land in the midst of these conditions wasn't an easy proposition, so his dad was thrilled to have a potential client call and ask to see a large ranch that was for sale. Our friend begged his dad to let him tag along for the appointment, and his dad agreed. They drove the client to the ranch land, and his dad began to give a tour of the property, doing his best to point out all its good qualities in hopes of minimizing how dry and burned the land was from lack of rain. Our friend decided to chime in and repeatedly said, "Dad! Dad! Dad! I want to say something!"

His dad finally turned to him and asked, "What, son? What do you want to say?"

And our friend replied, "I just wanted to say that IT LOOKS LIKE A DESERT OUT HERE!"

That's how he ended up being placed for adoption.

Not really. But his dad didn't make a sale that day.

I feel like life is like that ranch sometimes. We can be going along just fine, enjoying plenty of rain and things that give us life, and then before we even realize it's happened, we feel dry and burned out. Maybe it's a relationship that has run its course. Maybe it's our financial situation or an ongoing struggle with a coworker or family member. Whatever the case, we realize that part of our life feels like a desert.

When God showed Ezekiel the valley of dry bones, God knew why they were dry. They represented a nation that had turned from Him and cut Him out of their life. And when He asked Ezekiel, "Can these bones live?" Ezekiel replied, "O Lord God, you know."

Places and circumstances in our lives can appear to be nothing but dry bones. Some of them may be able to live again because God will breathe into them and give them new life if we just ask. But some things are so dry—or are making us so dry—that God is calling us to let them go so He can do something new. The key is that we have to ask Him for the wisdom to know the difference because only He knows what can live and what needs to die. And then we must trust Him to give us the strength to move from the desert to a place where our souls will feel refreshed and renewed and new life will spring forth.

Day 69

SELAH

··

I will remember the deeds of the LORD; yes, I will remember
your miracles of long ago. I will consider all your works
and meditate on all your mighty deeds. Your ways,
God, are holy. What god is as great as our God?

PSALM 77:11–13

I've always contended that King David may have been a little melodramatic. In the words of one of my favorite fictional characters, Moira Rose, "What you did was impulsive, capricious, and melodramatic. But it was also wrong." And I get it. I'd be a little overly dramatic too if I started out life as a shepherd and ended up being anointed king and spending years of my life being hunted by the current king, who was more than a little troubled.

Psalm 77:7–9 reads, "'Will the LORD spurn forever, and never again be favorable? Has his steadfast love forever ceased? Are his promises at an end for all time? Has God forgotten to be gracious? Has he in anger shut up his compassion?' Selah" (ESV).

And that word—"Selah"—used to confuse me. What does it mean? I know it's the name of a Christian group, but why? It turns out that *Selah* is a musical term that means to rest, to pause, to take a little break.

I have begun to realize that I have to build in times of rest when I am feeling overwhelmed and can't hear God or start to doubt if He's in anything

I'm doing. God can't speak when we are so busy serving Him that we forget to *rest* in Him.

The beginning of Psalm 77 is dramatic and full of the weariness we've all felt at one time or another. But then that "Selah" comes, and we see an entirely new perspective—after David rests and then stops his pity party in favor of remembering all that God has done. It's like David *knew* he needed to stop and rest and regroup.

What this tells me is that sometimes we all need a little Selah. Sometimes we need a place to pause and lift up our worries and fears and grievances and allow God to shift our perspective. And sometimes we just need to rest because, if we're going to be renewed, we have to be kind to our soul. We can't just keep going through the motions, pretending like it's all okay when it's not. It's okay to say we're tired and need a break.

Sometimes Selah is what we need to find our joy again and to remember all that God has done for us—and that what He has done before, He will do again.

Day 70

BEING A GOOD NEIGHBOR

································

"A Samaritan, as he traveled, came where the man
was; and when he saw him, he took pity on him. He
went to him and bandaged his wounds, pouring
on oil and wine. Then he put the man on his own
donkey, took him to an inn and took care of him."

LUKE 10:33–34

A couple different stories have been in the news lately about people standing by and doing nothing while someone around them was suffering and in pain. It has made me think of the quote by Edmund Burke: "All that is necessary for the triumph of evil is that good men do nothing." It's also been an opportunity for me to remind Caroline that to stand by and do nothing when someone is suffering and you are able to step in makes you as guilty as if you were the one causing the pain. I hope we never pass up an opportunity to show the people God places in our path what kindness, mercy, and compassion look like.

When Jesus tells the story of the good Samaritan, He talks about a man who had been stripped, beaten, and left for dead. A priest and a Levite, who were both considered holy men of that time, passed him by and ignored his pain. But it was a Samaritan, who was considered a social outcast, who took pity on the man.

The Samaritan not only took care of him in that moment but also left money for the innkeeper and asked him to look after the man until he was well. Jesus says that the Samaritan was the man who was the neighbor.

The thing is, we all have ways—both big and small—that we can be a good neighbor in so many areas of our life. It doesn't have to be as dramatic as rescuing a bloodied man on the side of the road (although that could be the case). It can be as simple as bringing a meal to a sick neighbor, stopping by the house of an elderly acquaintance to see if he or she needs anything, welcoming the kid who roams the neighborhood into your home for a cookie and a glass of milk, or listening to a coworker who is going through a hard time.

God has placed us in unique areas of our world where He calls us to be His hands and feet—to love the hurting, to take care of the sick, and to carry each other's burdens when we can't carry them alone. That's really what life is all about. Where can we help? Where can we make a difference? Where can we be a good Samaritan today?

I WILL BUILD YOU

···

"Afflicted city, lashed by storms and not comforted, I will
rebuild you with stones of turquoise, your foundations with
lapis lazuli. I will make your battlements of rubies, your gates
of sparkling jewels, and all your walls of precious stones."

ISAIAH 54:11–12

I'm always a little torn when I look back on my childhood. I can't say that it wasn't happy because at times it absolutely was beautiful and magical and all those things childhood is supposed to be in a perfect world. But there were also times when it felt scary and I felt alone and it was all a little shaky. My parents divorced when I was nine years old, and for a lot of years after that, life just didn't make sense.

It was during these years that we attended some odd churches. Or at least I remember them being odd. I mean nobody, like, danced with a snake or anything, but they were a far cry from the Catholic church where I spent the early years of my life. But it was at one of these churches that an older lady declared that Isaiah 54:11–12 was the passage that God showed her about my life, and I was encouraged and challenged. Actually, that's not true. I was more like, "Um . . . Okay, stranger that I don't know. Sure." Because I was probably about twelve and didn't really understand that God often uses the people in our life to speak things over us.

Years later, I remembered the words that lady spoke and read those verses with the eyes of someone with a little more life experience and realized how true they have been in my life. In fact, the older I get, the more I see how God has built my life, which seemed like it was in constant turmoil for so many years, into something beautiful. He took these broken pieces of my childhood and early adult life and used them to help me become who He created me to be—even when I didn't understand all that was going on and felt like there was no comfort to be found.

That's God's specialty. When times come in your life when you feel like an afflicted city and wonder if you'll ever feel okay again, when all hope is gone and you've buried your faith, you have a God who is using your pain to build something that is precious, something that will shine bright for the world to see.

Day 72

THE FRAGRANCE OF LIFE

....

For we are to God the aroma of Christ among
those who are being saved and those who are
perishing. To the one we are an aroma that brings
death; to the other, an aroma that brings life.

2 CORINTHIANS 2:15–16

So I have to tell you something that I wasn't sure I was going to admit publicly: I have hopped on the essential oil bandwagon.

I mean I'm not going to start selling them or anything crazy like that, but I have become a fan of diffusing a mixture of peppermint, lavender, and lemon throughout my home. I'm essentially one farmer's market trip away from the Basic White Lady Starter Kit™. But I love the way they make my house smell, and I've even discovered that if I put a few drops of lemon oil on a cotton ball and put it inside Caroline's soccer cleats, it eliminates the odor, which is basically a miracle.

The point I'm trying to make is that fragrance is a powerful thing. It can trigger memories, clear a room, or fill you with a sense of calm and well-being. And so it's interesting to me that Paul refers to us as being the aroma of Christ to both believers and non-believers. Through our words and actions, we essentially diffuse the fragrance of Christ's love to those around us, and it makes me realize what a privilege and responsibility it is to love others, follow where Christ leads, and do our best to make sure that we're not putting out an aroma that will cause people to be repelled by Christ instead of drawing them closer to Him.

And maybe, just like when I get the perfect blend of essential oils in my diffuser, if we're sharing Christ's beauty and love, people will look at our lives, smell something different, and want more of it in their own lives because they see how it permeates every part of us for the better. The sweet smell of the grace that has been poured out in our lives should be so powerful that it draws others in because they smell life—real, powerful, grace-filled life.

Day 73

DISCERNING GOD'S WILL

....

"Blessed are the pure in heart, for they will see God."

MATTHEW 5:8

If you're like me (I don't mean to assume you are, but if you're still with me on Day 73, then I have to think we may have some similarities), then it's likely that at times you face a challenging life decision and are really trying to discern what it is that God is calling you to do. Sometimes there isn't even a bad option as much as just trying to figure out which might be the *best*. And here's what happens in my life: I get it right about 50 percent of the time. The other 50 percent is when I jump in with both feet to something that seemed like what I should do . . . only to realize mid-jump that maybe I leapt before I really looked.

But here's what I love about God and what Matthew 5:8 promises us: "Blessed are the pure in heart, for they will see God." It doesn't say, "Blessed are those who never screw up" or "Blessed are those who do all the right things," because God is always more focused on our hearts than on our actions. We are flawed people just trying to do our best, and sometimes that's enough and sometimes we still fall short.

When the prophet Samuel went to look for the next king of Israel and saw David, God reminded Samuel that He wasn't concerned with outward appearance but looks at what is in a person's heart. If we allow ourselves to fall in love with Jesus completely and totally, we'll find more and more that our heart is in the right place, and that's when we experience the pure joy of what it means to walk in the way He has for us. Our desires for ourselves will line up more and more with His desires.

And that doesn't mean we become perfect. God is worried about us being perfect because He knows exactly who we are, with all our flaws and weaknesses. He's our creator and knows us better than we know ourselves. He wants our hearts to be pure because that's when we can really experience what it means to walk in the freedom of all that He intends for us to become. Yes, He wants us to live lives that are holy and pure, but He also is there to catch us when we inevitably fall short.

I PITY THE FOOL

···

Fools give full vent to their rage, but
the wise bring calm in the end.

PROVERBS 29:11

Um. So I have been a fool. Many, many times.

I am a feeler. I feel things deeply. I get annoyed in traffic, waiting in line, when someone does something dumb, when I think I've been offended, when someone says something wrong. And then there's the rage I feel when I forget to eat lunch and realize I'm starving at three o'clock in the afternoon. All of these can lead me to say things that seem to make me feel better in the moment but that I regret later.

The thing about anger and rage is that they make you irrational. I've said many things in the heat of an argument that I didn't even mean. That ugly part of me just wanted to make someone feel as bad as I feel in that moment or to have the last word. The problem is that I never feel good about it later. The last word often has an aftertaste that is nothing but bitter.

And so I'm trying to keep these words from Proverbs in mind and remember that the wise thing to do is to bring calm to the situation. This is especially helpful now that I have a teenage daughter who has her mother's tendency to vent all her grievances. I hear myself telling her all the things I have to tell myself: "Let's just wait a minute until you calm down" or "Maybe we need to stop and think about how the other person feels" or "You need to go to your room and take a minute and a few deep, cleansing breaths."

What I've finally learned after handling my anger and feelings the wrong way for many, many years is that I have never one time regretted taking a little bit of time to calm down, assess a situation, and not just blurt out my knee-jerk reaction to all the ways I think someone is stupid or wrong. It's amazing how a tense situation can usually be diffused if we respond to someone with love and patience and kindness instead of saying the first cutting thing that comes to mind in what is usually just a defense mechanism. When we quit basing our actions and decisions on pure emotion, it helps us make better choices in our relationships, which in turn gives us peace. And that peace protects us from the actions and words of others, from the enemy, and from our own selves making bad decisions that are based on emotions instead of reality.

Day 75

SHINE YOUR LIGHT

···

"In the same way, let your light shine before
others, that they may see your good deeds
and glorify your Father in heaven."

MATTHEW 5:16

We have recessed lights in our kitchen, living room, and dining room, which is essentially all one large space in our house. I'd draw you a picture of it, but I don't want to and it doesn't really help this story. Our house was built in the 1920s, so the recessed lights were a feature we added almost fifteen years ago when we had to have the whole electrical system updated. Turns out, it's inconvenient to have to turn off all the lights in your house in order to get enough electrical power to run the microwave, not to mention, you know, the safety issue of having wiring that was circa 1920 and maybe installed by Thomas Edison himself.

Over the last fifteen years, I haven't thought much about our lights. Perry makes sure to change the bulbs when one burns out but, other than that, they're a non-issue because they just do their job. You turn them on; they light up the room; the end. We're all familiar with what lights do, and I apologize that I just felt the need to write it down for you as if maybe you'd forgotten.

Anyway, several weeks ago, Perry decided to change out all of our existing bulbs with these bright white daylight LED bulbs he bought at Home Depot. I wasn't entirely sure I was going to be fan, but the moment he turned them on, it made such a huge difference in the way our rooms look. The colors are more vibrant, everything is so much brighter and lighter, and it honestly looks like we somehow made the house bigger. Friends have even come over and asked, "What have you done differently? You changed something." It's amazing the difference light can make.

And all of this has made me think about the light of Christ that shines in us. We can get used to it over time and take it for granted and forget how dark our life was before we experienced His light and love, but with each person we meet, we have the power in us to make a big difference in their life just by letting our light shine. We have been given all the power of Christ to shine brightly in this world, and it's been good for me to remember what a difference that light can bring to a dark place.

Day 76

MY OWN WORST ENEMY

···

But he said to me, "My grace is sufficient for you, for
my power is made perfect in weakness." Therefore I
will boast all the more gladly about my weaknesses,
so that Christ's power may rest on me.

2 CORINTHIANS 12:9

In the past week, a couple of things come up that have brought fears and insecurities to the surface that I thought I'd gotten past. It's jarring when you're
going along, thinking you're being your best self, and then BOOM—life rears
its ugly head and you discover you actually aren't a better person at all. Rather,
you'd just been in a season of life when things were pretty easy, which lulled
you into thinking you had everything under control. It kind of reminds me of
parenting because it's usually right when I think I'm doing a pretty good job at
this motherhood thing that Caroline does something that completely catches me
by surprise and makes me question everything I've ever taught her.

All that to say, I've spent the last few days beating myself up because in my
head I'm like, *Are we really back to this again? I thought that was old business.* It's
been a tangible reminder that anything I achieve in this life, any peace I have, any
semblance of goodness and self-control, is only there courtesy of the grace of
God. I will be my own worst enemy if you give me the chance.

And when I read the words of Paul in 2 Corinthians, I see that he wasn't that much different from me. I mean, other than that thing where he was beaten and in chains and wrote most of the New Testament. Other than that, we are practically the same. But Paul also had a thorn in his flesh that plagued him. In fact, he begged God three times to take it away before the Lord told Paul that His grace is sufficient and His power is made perfect in our weakness. This really works out for me because I have a lot of weakness at times. I worry too much about our financial situation, I am too fearful in my parenting, I am insecure about where I fit in certain groups, and I can be pretty selfish when I'm totally honest with myself. I'm not a fan of any of these traits, and so I pray that God will make me better.

However, I'm realizing that doesn't happen by Him just magically fixing these situations as much as it does when I trust Him to cover my weaknesses with His grace. God isn't about making us perfect, because He wants a relationship with us. And when we see all the ways we are flawed, we have the opportunity to put the focus back on Him and not on ourselves, realizing that His grace is sufficient for all areas in our lives. And if there is any good to be found in our lives, it will be by His power working through our weakness.

Day 77

VELVETEEN MOM

···

In the same way, the Spirit helps us in our weakness. We
do not know what we ought to pray for, but the Spirit
himself intercedes for us through wordless groans.

ROMANS 8:26

Now that I'm more than a decade down the motherhood road, I've realized
that being a good mom doesn't mean being a perfect mom. A perfect mom
puts sand in a plastic box so her toddler can have a meaningful sensory experience and doesn't care about the mess. A perfect mom plays board games for
hours on end and makes hot cocoa bars with candy cane stir sticks and makes
sure the milk is organic and the chicken nuggets are made only from chickens
allowed to roam free in sunlit barns. She never loses her patience, never checks
her texts while her child is around, and is the president of the parent/teacher
association while managing a Fortune 500 company before returning home to
prepare a delicious, nutritious dinner.

In short, the perfect mom doesn't exist. And if she did, we'd all hate her.

The perfect mom is a unicorn, mythical at best. But a good mom is the
velveteen rabbit, a little worn from use. And while I'm not confident in a lot of
areas, I'm confident that I'm a good mom— because what ultimately makes a good
mom showing up. I've held back hair as she's thrown up over the toilet and, I
regret to say, all over me. I've wiped her bottom and her feverish forehead.

· 174 ·

I've stayed in the school parking lot long after she's walked through the school doors, praying and hoping that today would be better. I've sat in the rain and the cold and in heat that rivals the surface of the sun to watch her play soccer. I've cried when she's overwhelmed by joy, and I've cried when disappointments have her down. I've yelled too much, lost my patience, and seen how many mornings I can get by with Frosted Flakes for breakfast. I've driven more carpools than I can count, attended Taylor Swift concerts, and spent many weekend nights with a houseful of tween girls with high-pitched squeals who think cleaning up after themselves means putting half-empty soda cans under the bed. I've looked at my phone too often, set the clock ahead an hour so I could tell her it was time for bed, and pretended to have an upset stomach just so I could have a few minutes alone in the bathroom.

But I have no doubt that she knows she is deeply loved because I have faithfully shown up for the job for the last fourteen years. It hasn't been perfect, it hasn't always been pretty, and nobody is likely to turn our story into an award-winning movie. Being a good mom doesn't really make the highlights reel because there is very little glamour in packing another peanut butter and jelly sandwich for lunch. It's just about being faithful with what has been entrusted to you for such a short time.

I could sob just thinking about it. It's loving hard, laughing loud, crying when you are at your breaking point, hugging them tight, and having a good bakery on speed-dial because there isn't any way you will be able to make a birthday cake like the ones the mythical unicorn moms post on Pinterest. And when I don't know what to do or how to handle a situation (which is often), I get on my knees and pray for wisdom, knowing that even when I don't know what to pray or what to ask for, the Spirit knows and is always interceding for me and for Caroline. Motherhood is messy, loud, beautiful, mundane, exhilarating, and gut-wrenching all at the same time.

But I wouldn't trade it for anything in the world.

MY SOUL WAITS

I wait for the Lord, my whole being waits, and
in his word I put my hope. I wait for the Lord
more than watchmen wait for the morning.

PSALM 130:5–6

I have a routine that I follow almost every weekday:

I wake up and gasp at the forty-five-year old woman staring back at me in the mirror.

Then I make sure Caroline eats something for breakfast while I pack her lunch.

After she leaves for school, I pour myself a cup of coffee and then sit on the couch with my dogs, Piper and Mabel, on either side of me, and that's where I stay for the next two to three hours while I catch up on email and write and sometimes watch an episode of *This Is Us* that I recorded the night before. Eventually, I get up and get dressed and usually go work out and run whatever errands I need to run that day, and then when I get back home, I load Piper and Mabel into my car and take them to the dog park to run.

I don't know if you're a dog person, but dogs are brilliant. And they learn a routine pretty quickly. Piper and Mabel know my daily schedule, and so as soon as I pull into the driveway after running my early-afternoon errands, they know that it's only a matter of time before I take them to the dog park. They follow me and whine at me and bark loudly every time I walk by the back door until

I finally can't stand it anymore and cave to their demands and their pleading puppy eyes. They wait for me. They put their hope in me. They wait for me more than watchmen wait for the morning, and I think people on the nightwatch are usually beyond thrilled to see dawn finally break.

And it makes me think about how I wait for the Lord in my life. Do I wait with an excitement and hope like Piper and Mabel wait for their trip to the dog park? Or am I missing out on all that He can offer because I so often forget to wait on Him and just run ahead to the next thing in my life? Do I spend too much time mired in disappointment instead of finding my hope in His presence and in His word? The honest answer is yes, but my dogs (of all the stupid ways I could learn something) have shown me what it looks like to wait with joy and anticipation, knowing that good things are always ahead when you wait on your Master and find your hope in Him.

Day 79

STONES OF REMEMBRANCE

....

Joshua called together the twelve men he had appointed from the Israelites, one from each tribe, and said to them, "Go over before the ark of the LORD your God into the middle of the Jordan."

JOSHUA 4:4–5

In Joshua 3, the Israelites were preparing to cross the Jordan River. Joshua had told them to consecrate themselves, "for tomorrow the LORD will do amazing things among you" (v. 5). It was the time of year when the Jordan River was at flood stage. Crossing it would be impossible unless God prepared the way. So as the priests stepped into the edge of the river, carrying the Ark of the Covenant, the water stopped flowing. The priests stood on dry ground in the middle of the Jordan—until the entire nation of Israel had crossed safely.

When they had reached the other side, the Lord said to Joshua, "Choose twelve men from among the people, one from each tribe, and tell them to take up twelve stones from the middle of the Jordan from right where the priests stood and to carry them over with you and put them down at the place where you stay tonight."

Joshua called the men together and explained what God had told him, and then he explained why:

Each of you is to take up a stone on his shoulder, according to the number of the tribes of the Israelites, to serve as a sign among you. In the future, when your children ask you "What do these stones mean?" tell them that the flow of the Jordan was cut off before the ark of the covenant of the LORD. When it crossed the Jordan, the waters of the Jordan were cut off. These stones are to be a memorial to the people of Israel forever.

I believe that we all need to have our own personal remembrance stones—stories of the times in our lives, from childhood through adulthood, when God built our faith, stone by stone, as He proved himself faithful over and over again, the moments He wove together my relationship with Him like a fine tapestry, thread by thread. When you look at the stones by themselves, they don't appear to be much, but when you put them together over the course of a lifetime, these stones of remembrance help you see that He is always true to His word and makes all things beautiful in His time. Restoration and redemption are always possible when we call on Him, and it's good to remember where God found us at whatever different stages of our life.

My remembrance stones are the stories I tell when people ask why I believe what I believe and why I trust in a God I cannot see. They are the stories I make myself remember when I can't see His hand. He is always building, always working, always giving us moments we can look back on and see that He is who He says he is and will do what He says He will do.

Day 80

HE NEVER LEAVES

We have heard of your faith in Christ Jesus and
of the love you have for all God's people.

COLOSSIANS 1:3-4

A few years ago, I was speaking at an event in Virginia Beach. The topic was marriage. My second book, *The Antelope in the Living Room,* is all about marriage, and for some reason people believe I'm some kind of expert.

And as I stood before that group of women, hopefully giving them at least one piece of helpful advice, I referenced the story of Gideon from the book of Judges. Then later I read a passage from Ezekiel where God promises that He will remove our heart of stone and give us a heart of flesh. Because sometimes that's the reality of what we need Him to do in our marriages, especially after the person we're married to the first five minutes of a trip to the soccer fields lecturing us on the importance of always refilling the washer fluid in the car.

Anyway, after the talk was over, they opened it up for a Q-and-A session. Which always makes me nervous because it means I may have to come up with something intelligent to say off the top of my head. But one woman, way in the back of the room, stood up and asked, "How did you come to a point where you rely on the Bible to help you figure out your life?"

I took a deep breath as I tried to figure out a succinct way to sum up why I look to the Bible for answers, why God is my very breath and life and the heart-beat of all that I am. But how do you even begin to explain that to a roomful of strangers? How do I describe the times He has rescued me, chased me, pursued me, loved me, healed me, and forgiven me?

Ultimately, I spoke words reminiscent of the chorus of "'Tis So Sweet to Trust in Jesus" and answered, "After growing up in the church, I spent a lot of time looking for things other than Jesus to make me happy. And none of them proved true. He has proven himself to me over and over throughout my life, even when I was faithless."

That's the short answer. But the real reasons are so deep that they are embed-ded into the very fiber of my being, moments when God met me in the middle of the mess I made and showed me the way back home, the times He pursued me while I was in a full out sprint in the other direction. He offers redemption where there has been destruction, grace where there has been failure, mercy where there is nothing left but broken bits and pieces of a life.

I nearly wrote that God finds us wherever we are and meets us there, but that's not true. He doesn't have to find us because He never loses sight of us. He is always there, waiting and loving and pursuing us as we go on our personal quests to find all the other things we think might bring us peace and fulfillment. As C. S. Lewis once said, "And out of that hopeless attempt has come nearly all we call human history—money, poverty, ambition, war, prostitution, classes, empires, slavery—the long terrible story of man trying to find something other than God which will make him happy."

God watches us, loving us, as we test and try and question and rebel—until the moment we fall like an exhausted child at His feet and tentatively ask, "Are You there?" And He replies, "I never left." He is always building, always working, always giving us moments we can look back on and see that He is who He says He is and will do what He says he will do.

OPEN MY EYES

··

Elisha prayed, "Open his eyes, LORD, so that he
may see." Then the LORD opened the servant's
eyes, and he looked and saw the hills full of
horses and chariots of fire all around Elisha.

2 KINGS 6:17

I have always been a fan of the *Rocky* movies. I know, with maybe the exception of the original *Rocky I*, that they are a little (or a lot) cheesy and formulaic, but I can't help but watch them anytime they're on. Rocky is always the underdog, and yet he always triumphs despite the unbelievable odds stacked against him. Bring it on, Ivan Drago and your Russian steroids. You don't even *know* that Rocky can train in Siberia and lift a wheelbarrow full of firewood, and that beats your fancy exercise machinery any day of the week. Mr. T? You think you're so tough? Not too tough for Rocky because he is going to train with his secret weapon, former frenemy, Apollo Creed.

And so I'm going to need you to make this leap with me from Rocky to Elisha in 2 Kings 6. Israel was at war with the nation of Aram, but God told the prophet Elisha what Aram's next move would be, and so Israel defeated Aram over and over again. But then the king of Aram found out that God was using Elisha to defeat him and so he sent an army to attack. Elisha and his servant woke up one morning to see that they were surrounded by an army, which is almost as bad as waking up and realizing you have to pack a school lunch and have nothing left in the pantry. Elisha's servant panicked. The odds weren't in their favor. In fact, it looked like certain defeat. But then Elisha prayed and asked God to open the eyes of his servant so he could see what was truly happening. All of a sudden, the servant could see that an army of angels was surrounding and protecting them from the attack.

I'm sure we've all had times in our lives when it feels like we are constantly in battle. We may be fighting against our own mind and the fears that creep in during the middle of the night, or it can be financial problems that seem to mount up or situations that arise with friends or family members. And we can start to feel like we're all alone in the battle and like there is no way we can possibly win the fight.

This is when I usually panic.

But we have the Maker of the universe fighting for us and angels protecting us at all times when we are in the midst of the battles in our lives. We just need to ask God to open our eyes so we can see all that is on our side and remember that, even though we can't see it with our human eyes, God is constantly protecting us and fighting for us.

And ultimately, that's even better than being trained by Apollo Creed.

HEY, IT'S ME

Jesus said to her, "Mary."
She turned toward him and cried out in Aramaic,
"Rabboni!" (which means "Teacher").

JOHN 20:16

Certain people in my life can call me on the phone and after I say, "Hello?" they can respond with, "Hey, it's me," and I know exactly who is on the other line. Their voices are as familiar to me as my own. I would know them anywhere because they are such a huge part of my life that I recognize them instantly. You probably have the same kind of people in your life.

On the third day after Jesus had been crucified, Mary Magdalene went to the tomb and saw that the stone had been moved. She ran to get Peter and the other disciples and told them what she had seen. They all ran to the tomb to discover that it was indeed empty, with nothing but strips of linen lying where Jesus had been. The disciples went home after this discovery, but Mary Magdalene stayed outside the tomb crying until two angels appeared. "Woman, why are you crying?"

She responded, "They have taken my Lord away." At this point, Jesus was standing there. But Mary didn't recognize Him as He asked why she was crying and who she was looking for. John tells us, "Thinking he was the gardener, she said, 'Sir, if you have carried him away, tell me where you have put him and I will get him'" (v. 15).

Then Jesus said to her, "Mary."

As soon as He spoke her name, she knew Him instantly. How many times had she heard Him say her name over the years? How many times since she had watched Him be crucified had she longed to hear His voice one more time? She immediately knew that the impossible had happened and that it *was* her Lord standing before her because she recognized His voice.

The thing about knowing someone merely by the sound of their voice is that it signifies how close you are to that person and how often you talk. It's a sign of intimacy. As I read the story of Mary Magdalene, I'm challenged to ask myself if I know the voice of my Lord as well as she did. Do I hear Him speak my name? Do I hear Him calling me to take a leap of faith? Do I invest in that relationship enough that His is one of the voices I immediately know when I hear it? Because that's the kind of relationship He wants to have with all of us, the kind of friendship where He can whisper our name and we know immediately that we are in the company of our Savior.

GODLY SORROW

··

Godly sorrow brings repentance that leads to salvation
and leaves no regret, but worldly sorrow brings death.

2 CORINTHIANS 7:10

Since I am a mom, I have a lot of standard mom lectures in my repertoire. These include such gems as "Don't Chew with Your Mouth Open," "Don't Just Stand There with the Refrigerator Door Open," and "That's Why I Told You to Bring a Jacket." I also have some more serious material such as "Are You Really Sorry or Just Sorry You Got Caught?" And I think that one is one that applies to so many situations as we read about celebrities and politicians who get caught in some sort of scandalous situation. We see them have to face the court of public opinion as they shed a few tears, and we wonder if they really see the error of their ways or if they're just quoting from a script that was given to them by their highly paid public relations person.

I believe that the words in 2 Corinthians sum it up best. When we have done the wrong thing and created a mess, do we experience godly sorrow or worldly sorrow? Godly sorrow recognizes that we have sinned against God, but also that He can bring restoration and healing, while worldly sorrow tells us there is no escape, no restoration, and that we are doomed. Godly sorrow brings healing and worldly sorrow brings death.

Look at the difference between Judas and Peter. Both of them betrayed Jesus leading up to His crucifixion. Judas delivered Him to the Roman soldiers for thirty pieces of silver, and Peter denied knowing Him three times out of fear. One of them hung himself in a field, and the other one went running to meet Jesus the next time he saw Him. What's the difference?

We see later that Judas regretted what he had done because he tried to return the silver pieces, but it was too late and he ended up taking his life due to his remorse. But then in John 21, we read about Peter being so overcome when he finally was in the presence of Jesus again that he jumped out of the boat to meet Him.

Judas felt remorse, but Peter understood repentance. That's the key.

God knows we are going to mess things up. Humans have been messing up God's plans and betraying His love from the dawn of time. It's in our nature, and we do it despite all our good intentions. Sometimes it's just easier to grab what we think we want instead of waiting for what He has for us. We want to do it our way because we have an enemy that knows how to make the wrong choice look so appealing that we can forget everything we know in one impulsive moment.

But here's what I know for sure: God never wants us to choose the sorrow of the world that leads to death because He is always pursuing us, no matter how far we've fallen, no matter how much we've messed things up, and offers us the chance to repent. And not only do we have the opportunity to repent, but He also redeems what we have broken because that's how much He loves us. He never one time gives up on us because He wants us all to live in such a way that we run to meet Him when we see Him, no matter how far away we've been.

DON'T SUFFER TWICE

"Can any one of you by worrying add
a single hour to your life?"

MATTHEW 6:27

The other night we watched the movie *Fantastic Beasts and Where to Find Them*. The main character is a quirky British guy named Newt Scamander, who has a briefcase full of all kinds of fantastic, magical creatures. He finds himself in New York City and—spoiler alert—chaos ensues. Imagine that. But in the middle of the movie, Newt Scamander says something that I've been thinking about ever since I heard it: "Worrying means you suffer twice." And I have found that to be so true, yet I still catch myself worrying when I'm in the middle of a situation where the outcome seems unclear.

It's human nature to want to know all the things that will happen over the course of a day, a week, or a month. It gives us this illusion of control if we can plan for scenarios A, B, and C. Sadly, life doesn't really work like that, and so we can find ourselves worrying about our finances, our marriage, our kids, our job situation, our health, our friends . . . and on and on. The list is really endless. But here's what I've found: most of the things I worry about the most never actually end up happening. And even when they do, they are almost never as bad as I imagined them to be. I totally get that bad things can and do happen all around us and to us, but worrying about all of those what-ifs doesn't change one thing—except for maybe our blood pressure and our stress level. And in all our worrying and imagining of worst-case scenarios, we never account for all the grace and mercy God will pour out in our lives if we do actually find ourselves in the middle of the worst thing we could have imagined.

I try to keep this in mind every time I feel myself begin to worry about situations I can't control. Life can be hard and scary, but worrying about this thing or that thing isn't going to be what gets us through any of it. Only when we keep our eyes on Jesus, knowing that He will work even the worst situations out for our good, is what can help us keep our perspective and faith in check. And like Newt Scamander says, "Worrying just means we suffer twice"—and that's while he was trying to keep a whole universe of exotic creatures contained in a briefcase while running around New York City. I mean, that's a lot going on.

So the next time I start to feel that familiar worry rise up in me like the fantastic beast it can be, I want to remember that God has me in the palm of His hand and that all that worrying isn't going to add a single hour to my life. However, trusting Him is going to make my life infinitely better and filled with peace.

Day 85

EVEN IF HE DOES NOT

....

If we are thrown into the blazing furnace, the God we
serve is able to deliver us from it, and he will deliver us
from Your Majesty's hand. But even if he does not, we
want you to know, Your Majesty, that we will not serve
your gods or worship the image of gold you have set up.

DANIEL 3:17–18

In December 2014, we all found out that my dear friend Jen's breast cancer was back with a vengeance. There is nothing like realizing that one of your oldest and dearest friends is facing death to shift your perspective and outlook on what really matters in life. So my best friend, Gulley, and I began to make visits to Dallas to visit Jen almost every chance we could find.

At that time, Mondays were her treatment days. We chose a Monday so we could sit with her at the hospital all day and keep her company. When we arrived at the hospital with our friend Jamie, Jen was getting an initial blood draw. They eventually moved us into what her nurse referred to as our own private "party room." That nurse seriously oversold what was basically a small patient room, but we were so thankful to have our own little place to set up camp with all our snacks and drinks and spend the day together.

And that's what we did. We laughed and told stories and solved problems and had ourselves a complete therapy session before the day was over. At some moments, I'd almost forget why we were there—until the nurse came in to do a blood draw or Jen's oncologist came in and handed her a "Cancer Sucks" pin to wear. That part? The part where we were all sitting in an oncology ward in a hospital? It still does not compute even years later.

The thing about being with dear friends is you can have fun just about any- where. This was never more evident than when Jen's nurse had to come in and tell us we needed to be a little quieter because we were laughing and talking too loud. It just goes to show that some things don't change even when one of you has cancer.

But our conversations grew more serious as the day progressed, and Jen was never one to dance around how she felt about something. She told us that this certainly wasn't the path she would have chosen for herself, yet she never once doubted the goodness and sovereignty of God over all of it. Jen quoted Shadrach, Meshach, and Abednego before they were thrown into the fiery furnace and had no idea if God would choose to save them from certain death. "If we are thrown into the blazing furnace, the God we serve is able to deliver us from it, and he will deliver us from Your Majesty's hand. But even if he does not, we want you to know, Your Majesty, that we will not serve your gods or worship the image of gold you have set up."

And I realized in that moment that that's what it looks like to truly put your faith in God, the faith my dear friend had even has she was facing her own death. It's easy when life is going along as planned, but what about when the "even if He does not" moments come? Do we trust Him then?

We lost Jen in August 2016, and though cancer had destroyed her physical body, her faith was stronger than anything I'd ever seen. She believed in the goodness of God until her very last breath here on earth, and I have no doubt she ran into His arms, knowing there was nowhere else she would rather be. Watching Jen's faith challenged me to trust Him more even when the hard times come, even when He doesn't do what makes the most sense to me, because He is sovereign and He is good.

THE REAL PROVERBS 31 WOMAN

·······································

She is clothed with strength and dignity;
she can laugh at the days to come.

PROVERBS 31:25

Here's a confession. I spent years just skimming Proverbs 31. Actually, I usually skipped it altogether because I knew the gist was the description of the wife of noble character, and frankly, it just seemed to highlight all my inadequacies. I have never one time selected "wool and flax" and worked with eager hands, unless you count how I shop online and can't hit the Purchase Now button at Anthropologie.com fast enough when there's a good sale. And I realize that Proverbs 31 is a goal and not a standard, but it still felt antiquated to me.

But then I read a commentary and found out something I had never learned in all those years of Sunday school and passing notes in the back row of church: many scholars believe that the words of Proverbs 31 were told by Bathsheba to her son Solomon. Remember Bathsheba? The one who was married to Uriah and took a bath on the rooftop, which led to committing adultery with King David? She discovers she is pregnant, King David places Uriah on the front lines of battle, where he is killed, and then the son Bathsheba gives birth to ends up dying in infancy. Bathsheba was a woman who knew heartbreak and deep sorrow.

She was a woman who could've easily decided she was past any sort of grace or redemption and that her life was too far gone for God to have any use for it.

Instead, Bathsheba repented and was faithful to God. She and David were blessed with another son they named Solomon, who became the wisest man of his time. Bathsheba was clearly an excellent mother and taught Solomon the value of wisdom and righteousness. I have to believe that Bathsheba was a big factor in Solomon becoming David's best son, surpassing his brothers, Absalom and Adonijah. And Solomon recognized the woman of character and strength his mother was because he wrote down her words in Proverbs 31, which epitomizes what it means to be a woman of virtue and strength. God took Bathsheba, with all her faults and failings, and made her into the Proverbs 31 woman. It's a story of redemption, a reminder that no matter what is in your past, you are never too far gone for God to make your life something beautiful.

And I think what I love the most is that in spite of all the terrible things Bathsheba experienced in her life—the loss of a child, her betrayal of her husband and his death, the guilt and shame of what she'd done—she found joy in God. Because it is only when we rest in the peace and joy God gives that we can laugh at the days to come—even when we've experienced the worst of days in our past. Because we know that God is the one who heals our wounds, wipes our tears, and redeems it all if we follow Him.

DON'T LIE ABOUT YOUR DOGS

....

Do not lie to each other, since you have taken off your old
self with its practices and have put on the new self, which
is being renewed in knowledge in the image of its Creator.

COLOSSIANS 3:9–10

A while back, I ran into Target for a few things. The problem is that there is no
such thing as a quick trip to Target because the store is designed to lead you
down endless rabbit trails. By the time I was ready to check out, I was starving,
so I found what appeared to be the shortest checkout line—except the guy in line
in front of me couldn't get his microchip card to work in the reader. (I get that
microchip cards are safe and secure and the wave of the future but—SERENITY
NOW—they never seem to work the same way twice.) Meanwhile, my stomach
was basically eating itself. Then I realized that the cashier in the line I chose is
one I have often. And this is where I need to tell you that she is very sweet and very
good at her job.

But here's the thing. Whenever I go to Target, I always buy these Dingo
chew sticks for our dogs, Piper and Mabel. And every time I have this cashier,
she rings up those Dingo chew sticks and then says, "AWWW! Do you have a
dog at home? What kind?"

I always smile and reply, "Yes, we have two dogs. They are Blue Lacys."

The problem is that this leads to a litany of questions. "What are Blue Lacys?" "What do they look like?" "What color are they?" "Are they friendly?" "Are they from the same litter?" "Do they get along?" "Did they vote for Trump?" And so on, until she forgets that she's supposed to be ringing up my purchases while we visit.

So when I realized it was this cashier, I prepared myself for the questions as she scanned the chew sticks and determined that, due to my starvation, I was not emotionally prepared for all the inevitable questions about Blue Lacys.

Sure enough, she looked up at me and said, "AWWW! Do you have dogs? What kind are they?"

Listen. I am the worst person you know. Because I looked right at her, thought about the most common breed of dog I know, and replied, "Labs."

I lied about my dogs to the cashier at Target. In my defense, I just wanted to get to Whataburger and had truly crossed the line into HANGRY territory. I didn't want to talk about my dogs. I just wanted to pay for my groceries and ten plastic coat hangers and two Mossimo shirts and be on my way.

However, my nefarious ways did not pay off because she proceeded to ask, "Awwww! What kind of Labs?" "How old are your Labs?" "How do you tell the difference between a Lab and a Golden Retriever?" "Are they from the same litter?" "Have you seen that movie about a Lab that plays basketball? Or was that a Golden Retriever?" "What are their names?"

So what I'm telling you is that lying never pays off. And this is a silly story that serves to confirm how dumb and selfish I can be, but it was a good reminder to me that it's always easier to just tell the truth. Sure, it can feel hard in the moment, and sure, it can lead to an uncomfortable conversation, but it gets the real feeling, issue, or problem out in the open so we can deal with it and move on. God, in His infinite wisdom, knows that speaking the truth with love and grace is going to be the very thing that leads to renewal in our daily lives, because when we live in the truth, we walk in His truth.

Day 88

WHEN YOU'RE
SEVENTY-FOUR

A heart at peace gives life to the body,
but envy rots the bones.

PROVERBS 14:30

I read an article the other day that essentially said that from the time a woman turns thirteen until she turns forty, it's basically downhill in terms of contentment and happiness. It's a slow and steady decline that not coincidentally begins to happen at a time when most of us are painfully self-aware and awkward. And in what is maybe the most depressing part of the entire article, it ended by saying that a woman's best chance at contentment is when she is seventy-four years old. I don't know about you, but I don't want to wait until I'm seventy-four to be feel content and secure in who I am.

I think the heart of it all is that our human nature causes us to spend a lot of time looking around at what everyone else has or does. We focus on all the ways they look better than us. And social media has made this infinitely worse because we have constant access to how great someone else's life looks compared to our own. It's so easy for envy and jealousy to creep in, causing us to lose any peace we have as we instead focus on what we lack instead of on what we have been given.

The great irony is that we often envy people who we really know nothing about—other than that they know how to filter a great moment on Instagram to make it look like what everyone wants. We don't know what they're going through, how they have been hurt, or the struggles they face. We sometimes never know the road someone else has walked to get to where they are or what they have ahead of them. If we did, our envy of what we perceive to be their perfect life might change.

Perry and I did high school ministry in our neighborhood for twelve years. It's a nice area of town, filled with beautiful homes and families that appear to be living the American dream. But what we learned over the years was that oftentimes what was on the outside didn't match what was going on inside the walls of that house. Inside was alcoholism, financial problems, marital difficulties, and parents who chose their money and career over spending time with their kids. It was a reminder that every single one of us is broken in some way, no matter how much we try to make it look nice and shiny on the outside.

When our focus shifts from envying others to seeing what God has for us and the unique gifts He has placed in our lives, we can experience real peace, real contentment, and real joy that isn't based on external things. And best of all, it doesn't require waiting until we're seventy-four years old.

Day 89

THE BEST NAP EVER

"I'll refresh tired bodies; I'll restore tired souls."

JEREMIAH 31:25 The Message

As I write this, we are almost at the end of the school year. Summer is so close that I can smell the Frosted Flakes that I will serve for breakfast when we finally roll out of bed long after the sun is up and the Coppertone we will slather on before we head to the pool for the rest of the day.

It's like I can see the finish line, but I'm so tired that I have no idea how we're going to make it there. We still have projects to finish and tests to take and soccer tryouts to complete. I have eighty-six different deadlines I'm trying to make, and all I really want to do is take a nap and then maybe watch some Netflix. I realize this sounds ambitious, but I like to have goals.

The thing is, we all reach points in our life when we're like, "Check, please. I believe I am done." But life still goes on, and there are lunches to make and groceries to buy and work projects that have to be finished and chicken that needs to be cooked for dinner before it goes bad and you have to throw it out.

Side note: I really want to make a joke about how you know when the chicken has gone bad—when it starts smoking cigarettes and wearing little black leather jackets. See? That's how tired my brain is right now.

We have a God who understands that life can wear us down. He made us to need rest, which is why all the health articles tell us we should be getting at least eight hours of sleep a night. We function better, we think more clearly, and our moods are infinitely better.

But often, it's not just our physical bodies that need rest; it's our souls. The physical tasks can wear us down, but it's often the mental and spiritual battles that feel like they're going to kill us. But God never meant for us to walk through them alone. He promised to refresh our weary souls. He knows the battles we face, that the daily grind and just life in general is hard, and so we just need to go to Him and ask Him to refresh the places in us that feel like they have reached an end.

Day 90

FAMILY PLANNING

Trust in the LORD with all your heart and
lean not on your own understanding.

PROVERBS 3:5

The other day I saw a woman wearing a shirt that read, "Oops! I forgot to have children!" across the front and I kind of wanted to run up and give her a hug while whispering, "You, madam, are my spirit animal." Except that would be weird on a lot of levels, so I buried that impulse. The truth is that I didn't forget to have children. I just had a child. One child. And lean in closer while I make this confession: my husband and I made that decision on purpose.

It's not what I'd planned when I was younger and daydreamed about my future family. In fact, I went through a phase in the mid-eighties when I imagined myself with five children named Mandy, Randy, Candy, Sandy, and Andy. You're thinking it probably all worked out for the best that I ended up having only one.

I certainly never envisioned myself being any kind of spokesperson for the only-child crowd, but over the last eleven years, as I've written on my blog, the question I get the most is whether it's okay to stop after one child and if I have regrets that we never gave my daughter, Caroline, a sibling.

It's a hard question. The number of kids you decide to have is an extremely personal decision, although you wouldn't necessarily know that by all the complete strangers who feel free to regularly ask, "So when are you going to have another one?" or "Don't you worry about what will happen when you die and she's left all alone in the world?" People are so great. And by that, I mean they can be extremely insensitive and can act like they have the right to get in your business even if you just met them on a plane or in line at Starbucks.

Honestly, we didn't officially arrive at the decision to have an only child until Caroline started kindergarten, and even then, I sometimes second-guessed our decision. Because what happens if we screw her up and end up two old people who have to spend holidays with just the dog? I'd Google articles about only children, reassuring myself that they often end up being higher achievers, leaders, and most importantly, not automatically in therapy over not having a sibling.

But I began to realize that while some of my concerns were legitimate, the majority were based on my perception of what a family was supposed to look like. However, when I blocked out the external noise, the well-meaning questions, and my own insecurities about people making me feel like I was less of a mom for having just one child and focused on how I felt and what was really best for our family, I found that I was completely secure in our decision and knew without a doubt that it's exactly what God intended for our family.

We often have this same experience with so many decisions in life. We are surrounded by people and a culture that wants to tell us who we're supposed to be, what we're supposed to do, and how our life is supposed to look. But Proverbs 3:5 doesn't tell us to trust in our well-meaning friends with all our heart to make our paths straight. We are called to trust in the Lord with all our heart and not to lean on our own understanding.

It's so easy to let our feelings or emotions in the moment make a decision that ultimately isn't what God wants for us but just feels right at that period of time. But when we keep our eyes and hearts focused on Him and block out that external noise, He promises to keep our paths straight, which is so much easier than when I find myself on a road I never should've traveled in the first place because I forgot to trust in what I know to be the most true.

Day 91

OPERATION HILL
OF BEANS

··

When the Philistines banded together at a place where
there was a field full of lentils, Israel's troops fled from
them. But Shammah took his stand in the middle of
the field. He defended it and struck the Philistines
down, and the LORD brought about a great victory.

2 SAMUEL 23:11–12

Second Samuel 23 begins by sharing the last words of King David and then goes on to tell us about David's mighty warriors, the men who were essentially the Special Forces of their time. They were the brave men who defended Israel time and time again in battle. And it's in the middle of this list that we read about Shammah and the stand he took in a field full of lentils, otherwise known as a field of beans. It's an easy anecdote to skip over because what is really that significant about fighting for a bunch of beans? I mean there's even a saying about something not being worth a hill of beans.

But I believe there's more to the story than meets the eye. The Philistines decided to attack the Israeli army in the middle of this field of lentils, and the Israeli troops decided to flee. But Shammah chose to take a stand right there in that field and defend it even though common sense says that a bean field probably isn't an optimal place to engage in a lopsided battle with the odds stacked against you. Shammah didn't compromise, he didn't back down, and he didn't decide that it wasn't worth all this trouble for just a bunch of beans. And I think that's because he knew it was a battle worth fighting and any ground he gave up to the enemy at that moment was going to be ground he'd have to fight like crazy to get back at some point or just accept that it was gone forever.

A time comes in all our lives when we have to make the decision to stand up and fight instead of backing down. We all have ground in our life that we will have to choose to defend, and it may seem at times that the ground we are called to protect isn't that significant, but that very ground is the ministry, the calling, the family, the path that God has given you, and so He has a plan and purpose for all of it. The greatest trick the enemy can play on us is to convince us that our marriage, our family, or our ministry isn't worth the fight. We have to hold our ground and remember that anything worth having is going to sometimes require us to stand where we are and not back down at the first sign of an attack.

And here's the encouraging part. Shammah took his stand in that field of lentils, but the scriptures tell us that it was the Lord who brought about the victory. The Hebrew translation of the name Shammah is "God with us," and so Shammah's faith was never in his own ability to fight the battle but that God was with him and would fight for him even though he was seemingly alone.

The next time we find ourselves facing a fight we didn't ask for or plan for—yet we know we are called to stand our ground—let's remember that our God goes before us and will fight for us. And sometimes what appears not to amount to more than a hill of beans is absolutely worth the fight if it's what God has put in our care.

Day 92

THE GOD WHO SEES

···

[Hagar] gave this name to the Lord who spoke to
her: "You are the God who sees me," for she said,
"I have now seen the One who sees me."

GENESIS 16:13

Here's the thing about life. It's going to be hard sometimes.

The end. Thank you for listening.

Feel free to have that calligraphied on a chalkboard.

The story of Hagar begins when God promises Abram an heir, yet his wife, Sarai, has yet to get pregnant after many years of trying. Sarai decides she's going to help God out and has her maidservant, Hagar, conceive a child with her husband, Abram. Shockingly, this plan doesn't go so well, and Sarai is terribly jealous of Hagar and mistreats her, causing Hagar to run away. Who could've seen that coming *besides everyone involved*? Yet I can't really judge Sarai because I too have made some really bad decisions in an impulsive move to help God out—because, you know, He's just the Creator of the universe and is probably in need of assistance.

Anyway, Hagar runs away with her son, Ishmael, and finds herself in the middle of a desert with no food or water. Hagar feels that all hope is gone when, suddenly, an angel of the Lord shows up. He tells her what to do, and she knows that God hasn't forgotten her. And so she gives God the name El Roi, which means "the God Who Sees." She is the only person in the entire Bible to give God a name. And I think it says so much about the heart of God that He met her there in the desert, in the midst of her hopelessness. Hagar was a minor character in the unfolding story of Abraham, yet in God's economy she was no less important. God saw her. And He provided for her.

I often feel like, considering the scope of all God has to deal with, my life is pretty small potatoes. I'm just a mom and a wife trying to love my family and love God and pack lunches and help with algebra homework. Does any of that really matter in light of all that is going on in the world?

But Hagar's story is a reminder to me that we serve El Roi—the God Who Sees. He sees all the small details of our lives. He sees our hopes, our dreams, our heartbreaks, our triumphs, and our struggles. He sees who we are, who we hope to be, and who we can become. It can be so easy to feel that we are overlooked as we just go about our daily activites like laundry, grocery shopping, and going to work—but we have a God who sees us.

And if we believe He sees us, then what's the point of stressing about figuring life out as if we're on our own? We don't need to have all the answers. We don't have to come up with a plan because we have a God who sees us and wants to be a part of everything we do and everything we are. He meets us in the deserts of our life and promises to give us everything we need.

HOLD YOUR PLANS LOOSELY

In their hearts humans plan their course,
but the LORD establishes their steps.

PROVERBS 16:9

My daughter, Caroline, is about to begin her freshman year of high school. I can't think about it for too long or I will quit typing and just curl up in the fetal position and hum "Sunrise, Sunset" to myself, which is really no good for anyone. She's also a soccer player, and we are finding out that if you want to play soccer at the college level, the process of sending out your player résumé and attending various showcases begins now. And so we've been having various conversations about what she wants for herself. Does she want to try to play college soccer? Would she go to a smaller school to play soccer and give up going to a larger university? What does she see herself doing as an adult?

I mean, I'm in my forties and I'm still trying to figure out what I see myself doing as an adult, so it's a lot to process for a fourteen-year-old girl. We were talking the other night, and I told her she is moving into the years when it is going to be so crucial for her to have her own personal relationship with God because she's going to have so many decisions to make. We talked about the importance of spending time reading the Bible and praying so that she'll really know how to discern the voice of God and where He's calling her to go—because ultimately, she's the only one who can do that. And it was in the midst of this discussion that she asked the million-dollar question: "What if God wants me to go somewhere or do something that doesn't feel like what I want to do?"

Yes. Good question. What *about* that?

Because haven't we all been there? I am such a fan of making my plans, charting my course, and getting ready to jump in with both feet right before I hear God whisper, "Um. That's not the way I want you to go. Trust Me." And sometimes? I keep going anyway. Those times are what I now refer to as My Life's Regrets. But the times I abandon my plan and surrender to His?

He has never done me wrong even one time.

And that's what I told Caroline as we talked. I said that we can make our plans and have our hopes and dreams, but we have a God who knows us even better than we know ourselves, so it's good to hold our plans with a loose hand. He knows the ways we can make a difference, the things that will truly make us happy, and what we need before we even know we need it.

As a mom, all I want for Caroline is for her to be exactly where God wants her to be because I know she'll be infinitely more joyful and content walking in His path for her life than in any path I can create for her. And it was a good reminder to me that I need to trust the One who knows her best as I'm teaching her to do the same.

Day 94

HOLY HYDRATION

....

"Let anyone who is thirsty come to me and drink.
Whoever believes in me, as Scripture has said, rivers
of living water will flow from within them."

JOHN 7:37–38

Last weekend Caroline had a soccer tournament in Houston, and we knew she'd play at least three games in the heat and the humidity that is Houston's trademark. Ever wonder what would happen if you put a swamp inside of an oven? Just visit Houston in the summertime and you will find out.

I've been a soccer mom for almost ten years at this point, so I know that hydration is key. You have to hydrate before you play in that kind of heat, and that means you have to start drinking plenty of water at least twenty-four hours ahead of the first game time, if not sooner. So I spent all weekend reminding Caroline, "Stay hydrated!" "Don't forget to drink your water!" "Did you finish that bottle of water?" Then she'd look at me, unscrew the lid to her water bottle, and take one tiny sip because she likes to see if my head will actually spin off my neck.

But the thing I know about hydration is you have to stay on top of it if you want to be at your peak performance level at game time. Once you realize you're not hydrated enough and start to cramp, it's too late. You're essentially done for the weekend at that point because your body can't really make up the deficit no matter how much you drink. You have to prepare ahead of time. And so I have just accepted that I will spend two-thirds of my life reminding my daughter to "Hydrate! You have to hydrate!"

What dawned on me this past weekend is that our relationship with Christ is a lot like being hydrated for a soccer game. We need to be in daily communication with Him through reading our Bible and praying because that is what fills us with His love and power. When we are full of God's love, we are living our life at peak performance because we are looking for ways to be His hands and feet right where we are.

There have been times in my life when I get too busy, too distracted, or just tired of spending time with Him. I let myself get depleted, and then when a challenge comes or a hard time hits, I don't have any reserves to draw from, and so I find myself drained and scared and tired. Jesus is our Living Water. He is the only thing that can truly fill us up and help us live the life He intended us to live. And when we continually allow that Living Water to be our focus, we can't help but let it overflow to those around us. We weren't made to operate from a place of depletion, and He is always waiting, ready to fill us up, and He's the only thing that can satisfy every hope, dream, or longing we have in our hearts.

Day 95

STEPPING UP AND STEPPING IN

···

"Truly I tell you, whatever you did not do for one
of the least of these, you did not do for me."

MATTHEW 25:45

One night, when Caroline was about nine, Perry was in the backyard grilling steaks. I pulled out the placemats and began to set the table. I put forks and sharp steak knives for Perry and me but only a fork at Caroline's place. As we began to eat, Caroline asked, "Hey, where's my knife?" I offered to cut her steak as Perry looked at me and said, "You know I let her skin and butcher the deer she shot at the ranch last weekend, right?" Um, no. I did not know that because that is terrifying.

In that moment, I realized the fundamental difference between what moms and dads do. Dads tend to encourage kids to take risks, accept challenges, and assert their independence. A quote by Erin Hanson says, "There is freedom waiting for you on the breezes of the sky, and you ask 'What if I fall?' Oh but my darling, what if you fly?" Moms worry about the falling, and dads are the flight school instructors.

We found out we were having a girl when I was about twenty weeks pregnant, and from that moment on, certain people asked if Perry had hoped for a boy. Perry's answer was always the same,: "I can do anything with a daughter that I could do with a son." And that's what he's done. I call them Big and Little Enos (I am never afraid of a *Smokey and The Bandit* reference) because Caroline is his mini-me. He's taught her how to hunt, how to fish, and how to throw a baseball *and* a punch. He's pushed her to take risks, try new things, and never accept that she can't do anything she sets her mind to do. In a world where dads are sometimes expendable, Perry has been a constant champion for Caroline, and she hasn't had to wonder even a moment if she is loved and adored. He is the very definition of steadfast and loyal.

But here's the thing. Perry lost his own dad in a plane crash when he was just nine. That's a tender age to lose one of the most important people in your life. And Perry's dad was great, full of life and love and thirst for adventure and fun. Perry was left with a huge void. Sure, he had the lessons and love his father had instilled in his first nine years, but what about after that?

I'll tell you what happened. Men in the community stepped up to fill in the gap. They took him hunting and fishing; they taught him to look someone in the eye and give a firm handshake; they imparted what it means to give your word and the importance of standing for what you believe in. They modeled love and loyalty to their families and included my husband in trips and activities where he could find adventure and face challenges. All these years later, he'll tell a story at dinner—as we all sit around with our steak knives—about something Jim Martin said or the time Mr. Holzhausen did that or how Mr. Swank taught him to do this.

Two weeks after Perry lost his dad, his mom sent him to summer camp as planned in an attempt to keep life as normal as possible. While he was at camp, he got hurt and ended up in the camp infirmary. As the young camp nurse bandaged him up, she tried to distract him by making conversation. "So what does your dad do?" Perry answered matter-of-factly, "My dad died two weeks ago." I think we can all safely assume that that poor camp nurse is still in therapy over that exchange. But it was an early indicator of how Perry took one of the worst possible events and chose never to feel sorry for himself. He says he never felt cheated that he lost his dad so young because he was surrounded by so many wonderful men who stepped up to the plate.

I watch the way Perry effortlessly loves, equips, and challenges Caroline to be the best version of herself, to make sure she's ready to fly, and I am forever grateful to the men who showed up in his life. They helped him become the man and father he is today, and we wouldn't trade him for anything in the world. I look at the way God used those men in such a powerful way, simply because they were willing, and realize that God can use each of us in someone's life, even if it just looks a lot like a fishing trip.

FLY AWAY

Cast your cares on the LORD and he will sustain
you; he will never let the righteous be shaken.

PSALM 55:22

The last few months have been filled with a lot of stress. Some of it is just normal day-to-day stuff, but I've had a bunch of deadlines to meet, relationships to navigate, financial issues to figure out, and on some days, all these things have seemed to converge at once, and I kind of want to run away. I think that's why Psalm 55 caught my eye a few days ago: "Oh, that I had the wings of a dove! I would fly away and be at rest. I would flee far away and stay in the desert."

Yes. Sometimes I wish I had the wings of a dove and I could fly away and be at rest. However, I would not flee and stay in the desert. I would prefer a nice five-star resort where I can lay by a pool as people bring me drinks and food and cool towels spritzed with cucumber water. But I guess the Psalmist didn't know about that option and so he chose a desert instead.

Tomato, to-mah-to.

But even though the Psalmist and I disagree about where we would like to flee, Psalm 55 shows that stress and troubles leave us feeling the same today as they did thousands of years ago. We have all had times where our hearts have been broken, our troubles seem never-ending, and even people we thought were our friends have turned on us. Even the good things in our life can sometimes add to our stress level. We worry about our kids, our marriages, our jobs, and our world. It can all begin to feel like too much.

And those are the times I need to take a deep breath and remember that when it all starts to feel like it's coming undone, I have a safe place to turn. As it says in Psalm 55:8: "I hurry to my place of shelter, far from the tempest and the storm."

God alone is our shelter and our strength. Our world may feel scary and fragile, but He promises that the righteous will never be shaken. If we keep our eyes on Him, if we trust Him in all our ways, He will give us the strength we need to get through whatever life throws our way. He is our strength and our sustenance, and He never meant for us to handle all of life's problems on our own. And maybe that's even better than a five-star resort.

GOD'S WORK OF ART

Consider it pure joy, my brothers and sisters, whenever
you face trials of many kinds, because you know
that the testing of your faith produces perseverance.
Let perseverance finish its work so that you may
be mature and complete, not lacking anything.

JAMES 1:2–4

I was scrolling through Instagram the other day because that is my general go-to activity any time I find myself waiting in line at the grocery store or sitting in a waiting room somewhere, and I saw this picture someone posted of the beautiful pieces of sea glass she and her kids had found on the beach that morning. Since I have spent most of my life going to Texas beaches, I am not as familiar with finding sea glass as I am with finding tar on my bathing suit. Sea glass is infinitely preferable.

Many years ago, before we knew about the importance of things like protecting the environment and taking care of Planet Earth, people used to feel free to throw their trash into the ocean because I guess they assumed the ocean was vast enough to be their own personal Dumpster? Or like trash just went out to the part of the ocean no one ever sees? I don't know. But if you're a child of the seventies like I am, you might remember the commercial that featured the crying Native American who was sad about all the litter across America.

He scared me straight.

Anyway, all those bottles that were tossed in the ocean over the years end up being broken into shards of glass as they are pounded by the waves. They are tossed about and hit sand and rocks and these sharp, jagged pieces of glass eventually get polished into smooth, polished pieces that look like jewels and are little treasures that wash up on the beaches.

When I saw that picture of my friend holding all that beautiful sea glass, it made me think about how much we are like all those broken pieces of glass. We have sharp edges, we are broken, and certain parts of our lives make us feel like we are beyond usefulness or purpose. But God uses the waves and the rocks in our lives, the obstacles that often seem like they are going to be the final straw that will break us, to create something new and even more beautiful than what we once were.

He hones out our sharp edges, polishes our hearts, and makes us into His very own beautiful works of art. Because it's often after we've gone through the hardest situations and trials that we are the most effective and best version of ourselves and God is able to use us in other people's lives to encourage them and sustain them as they go through hard times. And it helps us to remember in our own lives that when difficult times come, we have a God who makes all things beautiful in the end.

Day 98

HEART EYES

··

I pray that the eyes of your heart may be enlightened in
order that you may know the hope to which he has called
you, the riches of his glorious inheritance in his holy people,
and his incomparably great power for us who believe.

EPHESIANS 1:18–19

For many years in my late teens and early twenties, I bought expensive sunglasses for myself. I felt like having that Ray-Ban insignia on the lens was imperative and somehow chose to ignore the fact that maybe someone earning just over minimum wage should spend her money more wisely. I also inevitably ended up losing and/or breaking the sunglasses because I am really not a person who can have nice things—particularly nice, fragile things that are fairly small. Then in my thirties I had a child who liked to break sunglasses as a hobby, and so I gave up on nice sunglasses. My sunglass criteria essentially became any pair with enormous frames that were less than $14. Basically, I turned into my grandmother.

And truly, my cheap sunglasses and I have lived together in peace and harmony ever since. I no longer suffer sunglass stress because even if I leave them on a table in a restaurant or crush them when I sit on them in the seat of my car, I'm only out $14. I have felt like they sufficiently meet my sunglass needs and I can see everything I need to see.

But then I went on a fishing trip to the coast with Perry and Caroline. They regularly go on fishing trips together, but we decided it might be fun to go as a family. As we drifted through the shallow water, Perry and Caroline kept pointing out various fish they could see, and I'd pretend I saw them too. But the truth was I had no idea what they were looking at because I just didn't see it.

Perry finally said, "You can't see anything with those cheap glasses, can you? Try these." He handed me his super nice polarized fishing glasses. It was like I was Dorothy Gayle and had just been transported from Kansas to Oz. My eyes could suddenly see a whole world under the water that hadn't been visible just a few minutes earlier when I had on my $14 sunglasses. It made me wonder what else I'd been missing all these years because I didn't have the right equipment to enhance what was right in front of me.

It's just like that with the eyes of our hearts. We can start to feel so discouraged or disheartened because we can only see what's right on the surface of our lives, dreams that haven't come true, heartbreak that never seems to end, or financial strains that weigh us down. But our hope isn't in any of what we can see right now, these temporary things that ultimately won't amount to anything in the scheme of eternity. The hope to which we've been called is so much greater, deeper, and more powerful than anything we can fathom or understand until we're able to see it through the lens of how big our God is and the incomparable riches He has for us when we trust in Him.

Day 99

EVERY PRAYER
IS ANSWERED

....

"Ask and it will be given to you; seek and you will find; knock and the
door will be opened to you. For everyone who asks receives; the one
who seeks finds; and to the one who knocks, the door will be opened.
Which of you, if your son asks for bread, will give him a stone? Or if
he asks for a fish, will give him a snake? If you, then, though you are
evil, know how to give good gifts to your children, how much more
will your Father in heaven give good gifts to those who ask him!"

MATTHEW 7:7–12

I've thought a lot lately about the times in my life when I've asked God for
something and He hasn't answered my prayer the way I hoped he would. I
mean, this is clearly a prevalent thing because Garth Brooks even sang a song
about it in the early nineties. It's one of the great mysteries of life when you look
at the prayers God answers the way we want versus the prayers that seem to not
have an answer or have been answered in a vastly different way than we hoped.
When my dear friend Jen was dying of cancer, we all prayed faithfully that she
would be healed and whole, and God chose to answer that prayer by bringing
her to heaven. And though I am so glad she isn't in pain any more, we miss her
so much. It's hard to understand why God chooses to heal one person's physical
body and decides that another one's time on earth is through.

The truth is that every prayer we offer to God is answered. It's just that sometimes those answers look different than what we were expecting. We can feel like we asked for bread and were, in fact, given a stone. But I'm learning more and more as I settle into middle age (yikes) that I often learn the most in the empty places. I can tend to fill my life with all kinds of things in an attempt to make myself feel content and happy and then discover that none of it has filled the deepest ache in my heart. It's often coming face-to-face with my own insufficiency where I discover again that only God can sustain me through the seasons of life where answers to prayers don't seem to come as quickly as I'd hoped or in the form I expected.

God does something in the emptiness of our lives. He refines us, comforts us, and His Word promises that He is a Father who gives us good gifts. He isn't going to give us a snake instead of a fish, and for that I am eternally grateful. He sometimes uses the places in our lives that are the most vulnerable to show us that He is true and just and faithful and that He alone sustains us. Ultimately, His love for us is the greatest answer to prayer of all. He isn't going to abandon us or leave us longing. It's just that He is always interested in the greater goal than the short-term solution of giving us exactly what we think we want—only for us to discover later that it's not what we really wanted at all.

It's like the Christmas when Caroline claimed that all she wanted was a glow in the dark Wubble ball (As seen on T.V.!). I knew from reading through reviews that it was a waste of money and wasn't nearly as amazing as what she'd built it up in her mind to be. I didn't want her to settle for a Wubble when I knew there were better gifts out there waiting for her.

The times in my life when I am truly seeking God, when I'm passionate about drawing closer to Him and letting Him fill my life with His glory and His love, are the seasons I look back on as the ones that taught me the most about who He is, how much He loves me, and how He withholds no good thing from us.

FOR SUCH A TIME

Who knows but that you have come to your
royal position for such a time as this?

ESTHER 4:14

Afriend of mine recently decided to take a mission trip because she felt like God was calling her to do something outside her comfort zone. And as I listened to her process this decision, I began to wonder if God wanted me to do something different. My life feels pretty ordinary and mundane in the whole scheme of things. I go to the grocery store, I do laundry, I pack school lunches, I cook dinner, and I drive my daughter to sixty-four different activities each week. It's easy for it all to feel insignificant.

Because you know what nobody wants to make a movie about? A normal, average life where you do your best to love your husband and your kids and show up to work every day.

But here's the thing about God. He often uses the most unlikely people and scenarios to accomplish His purposes. When we read about Esther in the Bible, we learn that she was raised by her cousin, Mordecai, and when she was a young woman was taken to King Xerxes' palace for a year of beauty treatments in preparation to meet the king. (Side note: I can get on board with a year of beauty treatments. I looked in the mirror this morning, and I have apparently angered the region between my eyebrows because it is extra wrinkly right now.) The beauty treatments combined with Esther's natural charm and beauty worked. King Xerxes made Esther his new queen. And so this Jewish orphan girl found herself in an incredibly unique position, with one problem: her new husband didn't know she was Jewish.

It was right after this that an evil man named Haman came up with a plot to get the king to destroy the Jewish people, so Esther's cousin, Mordecai, asked her to intervene with King Xerxes. And now we have another problem: the king hadn't summoned Esther in thirty days, and it was dangerous to the point of life-threatening to go to a king who hasn't requested your presence. Yet Esther risked her life and her position to save her people.

One brave girl in the right place at the right time saved an entire nation from being annihilated. One brave girl who wasn't afraid to speak up changed the course of history.

Our lives may lack some of the drama of Queen Esther's, yet there is no doubt that God has placed us where we are, in this time and in this generation, for such a time as this. People all around us in our communities, our schools, our workplaces, and our families are in desperate need of God's love and mercy and grace. We live in a world that needs bold people to proclaim the difference between God's truth and the lies that this world will try to sell us. Can that feel scary? Absolutely. But is it worth it? Always.

God took a Jewish orphan and made her queen of a vast empire. Esther was nobody special and yet became a woman we still talk about today because she used her life to make a difference.

It's a reminder that God uses unlikely, ordinary people to accomplish His divine purposes. Maybe you're wondering if you're the exception? Could God possibly use *you*, with all your brokenness and imperfections? With your exact talent or influence? I have no doubt that the answer is yes.

He is a God who specializes in using the ordinary, daily acts of faithfulness to change the world around us. We only have to be willing. We only have to be everyday holy.